Contents

Preface

This is a 'how-to' – not 'do-it-yourself' – guide to your legal and financial responsibilities as an entrepreneur and employer: how to start your business, how to keep it going and how to avoid the legal pitfalls that beset your path. You are forewarned and forearmed but *not* equipped to be your own lawyer.

Chapter 1 outlines business structure. Later chapters deal with the impact of your choice of structure on various aspects of your business dealings. Some land, tax and insurance law and relevant areas of commercial law are covered as well as health and safety and employment legislation and litigation.

This is, however, a slimmed-down, easy-reference edition of the original *Law for the Small Business* and the law is set out in broad terms. If you run into problems you must dig deeper and consult legal and/or financial experts.

But the pile of legislation daily grows higher. In many areas ignorance is no defence and you cannot afford to risk yourself and your capital in the legislative jungle without some knowledge of the terrain.

A general note: our law is now part of the commercial and social law of the European Union, a common market for capital, labour and goods. EU law applies directly in the member states and cannot be altered or amended by reference to our earlier or later legislation. Common standards of quality and safety are being imposed on goods and services, procedures are becoming more open and increasing attempts are being made to reduce burdens on the smaller business.

The law stated is at March 2001 but the date label on the law is no indication that it is in force. If in doubt, seek legal advice. Your local Citizens' Advice Bureau, Consumer Advice Centre, trade or employers' association or Chamber of Commerce may be able to advise you and various government departments publish useful and informative pamphlets.

1

Starting out

Going into business can be simple enough but the financial implications are complicated. Independence is tempting, partnership has its pitfalls and behind the facade of many a private limited liability company is an entrepreneur as fully exposed to outrageous business misfortune as the sole trader.

The choice of business structure, however, is essential to the way you operate. It is the legal framework within which is determined your share of profits and losses and your responsibilities to associates, employees, creditors and anyone investing in your expertise.

Choices

Sole trading

The sole trader is the ultimate entrepreneur. You put your own money on your own expertise, taking out and putting into the business as much money and time as you choose and you are financially committed to the extent of everything you own. If you fail, creditors can demand payment in full, seizing and selling everything you own, including personal possessions.

Personal assets can be put beyond the reach of business creditors – for instance, assets can be put into relatives' names with the proviso that they invest in the business – but this reduces flexibility. They may not stand by you and transferring the family home into your spouse's or partner's name can be disastrous if you end up in the courts. Also, there may be liability for tax and/or stamp duty and some transactions can be set aside if you go bankrupt. You should therefore seek expert advice before taking action.

Partnership

Partners share problems and profits but the price may be high. The partnership is not a separate legal 'person'. Partnership law is being reviewed, particularly the problems arising from lack of independent legal personality, the break up of the business on change of ownership and the partners' unlimited liability, but currently you, your partners and the business stand or fall together and an insolvent partner can put the partnership out of business. Partners are jointly liable for all the partnership's commercial obligations, although you are responsible only for your partners' dishonest acts if you are involved in them. When you leave the partnership, you take financial responsibility with you unless you publicly announce the split by notifying business contacts and advertising it in the official *Gazette*.

Partnerships can be based on oral, informal agreements but the law puts a full agreement together if details are not specified. It is therefore best to have a formal, signed and witnessed, agreement. This sets the pattern of your current and future financial life and you should take legal advice before finalising it, so that you and your partners fully understand its implications.

Sleeping partners have the same liability as other partners even if their only involvement is investment in the business in return for a share of profits.

Limited partnership

Partners can put limits on financial commitments but at least one partner must have unlimited liability for business debts. The limited partner has limited rights and can only give general advice, and involvement in the business brings unlimited liability. Essentially the position is that of a lender to the business receiving interest at a rate varying with profits. But the limited partner is not a creditor and can only resign with the other partners' consent, unless other arrangements are agreed.

Limited partnerships must be registered with the Registrar of Joint Stock Companies at the Department of Trade and Industry, who must be notified of changes within 15 days. Details of the limitation and/or change must also be sent to the Companies Registrar and the *Gazette*.

Limited liability partnerships (LLPs)

LLPs are a new form of corporate business structure organised like a partnership, but where the members (partners) have limited liability. They have certain duties, including those usually carried out by company directors or secretaries – for instance, signing and filing annual accounts and putting together the statement of business affairs in insolvency.

Disclosure requirements are similar to a company's, including the requirement to file annual returns and notify changes in membership, changes of members' names and addresses and a change in the Registered Office address.

Like companies, LLPs are legal entities separate from their members, so the LLP is liable to the full extent of its assets and members have limited liability. Third parties will usually contract with the LLP rather than with members, but individual members may, in some circumstances, be liable for negligence.

Incorporation is achieved by registration at Companies House and costs £95. Members provide the working capital and share the profits. Income is treated similarly to partnership. The LLP is taxed as a partnership and members pay Class 1 and Class 4 NICS.

Partnerships converting to LLPs receive relief from stamp duty on property transferred in the first year, subject to conditions. New and existing partnerships of two or more persons can incorporate as LLPs but not an existing company.

Franchising

A franchise agreement licenses the franchisor's goodwill through a partnership agreement with the franchisee, who can be a sole trader, partnership or company. The franchisor gives ongoing support and advice, licensing a package of rights – for instance, copyrights, patents and know-how –

and monitoring the franchisee, mainly by financial and quality controls. The franchisee pays a fee plus royalties and/or dividends. The franchisee owns the business but must conform with 'house-style' and the franchisor has ultimate control.

The franchise agreement must comply with both UK and EU law relating to unfair competition, and restraint of trade and the law is complicated. You are therefore advised to consult specialists in the field.

Limited companies

Trading as a private limited liability company enables you to enjoy the profits of the business while distancing yourself from its debts and obligations. The company can be formed with one shareholder/director but he or she cannot also be the company secretary.

Incorporation

Incorporating business activities brings the business to life as a separate legal person. Corporate structure facilitates outside investor participation and expansion. Debts are the company's debts and business goes on in spite of the resignation, death or bankruptcy of management and shareholders.

The fastest route to incorporation is to buy a ready-made 'off-the-shelf' company from a registration agent or Companies House. Existing shareholders resign in favour of your shareholders and you appoint your own director and secretary. You can change the company name but first check to see that the 'objects' clause of the Memorandum – which covers the activities of the business – fits your business.

You can register a brand new company with Companies House but it involves delays, extra documentation, expense and advertisement in the *Gazette*. The ready-made procedure is straightforward and faster but there are technicalities and you should seek professional advice before buying.

The Memorandum and Articles of Association

Your company is 'limited by shares' and the Memorandum states you are in business to make a profit and that the liability of the members (shareholders) of the company is limited to the nominal value of their shares. The Articles set out the shareholders' rights and obligations.

Directors, shareholders and limited liability

Whoever subscribes for and holds company shares must pay the company for them and responsibility for company debts is limited to the nominal (face or par) value of their shares. If they are fully paid up, the company cannot call on them again, even if the business is insolvent. It is the directors and management who are responsible to the company, shareholders and creditors but, unlike sole traders and partners, only in specified circumstances. If they do not go beyond the limits of the authority given by the company's Memorandum and Articles and act honestly and reasonably, creditors' claims can only be made against company assets.

Unlimited company shareholders are liable for all company debts, although creditors must go to court before they can obtain payment. Small limited companies can now file unaudited accounts with Companies House and do not have to file a directors' report, so the dispensation absolving unlimited companies from the requirement to file certain reports and accounts is less attractive.

EU law

Community law applies directly in the UK and cannot be altered or amended by reference to our own earlier or later legislation. Changes to our company law mainly apply to public companies but community law has had and continues to have a major impact on our commercial and consumer legislation.

Loans

Sole traders can reduce or increase business capital as they please. Partners can borrow and lend to the business as agreed among themselves. Some complicated legal provisions, however, stand between company directors and business capital for loans over £5,000 and sometimes they also need the shareholders' consent (see pages 144–45).

When the business borrows money, sole traders' and partners' contingent liability – that is, their ultimate responsibility for business debts – is enlarged accordingly. Loans to the company do not affect the directors' and shareholders' contingent liability and additional shareholders and debenture-holders buy a share of existing and future profits but, like any other lender, their only claim is against company assets.

Retaining control

Partnership or company, the majority rules the business. The junior partner, however, is in a stronger position than a minority shareholder and majority shareholders can often ride roughshod over the objections of minority shareholders and dissenting directors. Unless otherwise agreed, the resignation of dissenting partners dissolves the partnership and in some circumstances a partner can only be bought out or forced out in accordance with the terms, if any, set out in the partnership agreement.

Formalities

Sole traders and partnerships trading in their own names can simply open their doors for business. Paperwork and administration are their own – and the VAT and tax inspectors' business – and the partnership agreement is mainly for the protection and information of the partners.

Partnerships and companies must present accounts in a prescribed form, have an annual audit and keep certain registers. Companies must file accounts and annual returns, listing changes made during the year, with the Companies Registrar. Unlimited companies do not have to file reports and accounts but they must send in the annual return. Documents filed with the Registrar are available for public inspection. There is therefore some inevitable publicity for even the smallest company.

Dealing with Companies House

You can now incorporate your limited liability partnership or company by filing the necessary documents electronically through incorporation agents. After incorporation you can register your business name and keep Companies House informed electronically yourself and download company and other searches. Details of the system can be found on the Companies House Web site (www.companies-house.org.uk).

Close companies

There is a tax disadvantage for family and director-controlled companies controlled by up to five 'participants' and their 'associates'. Associates include family and nominee shareholders. Participants – that is, anyone with a claim to the company's income or capital – pay additional income tax on some fringe benefits and both participants and associates are liable for income tax on loans.

If loans were made to participators during an accounting period you must notify the Revenue that the company is a close company and there could be liability to tax.

Tax comparisons

Sole traders, partners, directors and partnerships pay income tax; companies pay corporation tax. Trading on your own account takes assessment to tax from Schedule E to Schedule D, from the category of an employee to the self-employed. Schedule E taxpayers are taxed at source under PAYE and must fight for tax concessions after tax has been deducted. The Schedule D taxpayer has more control over income, outgoings and tax and, if well advised, can usually retain more earnings.

Sole traders and partners pay the lower self-employed rate of National Insurance contribution in Class 2 and Class 4. Company directors pay Class 1 contributions as employees and the company contributes as employer. The amount is a percentage of income and varies depending on whether or not the employment is contracted-out.

Sole traders and partners are personally liable for tax on business profits. The company is responsible for its own tax bill and, unless it is a close company, directors and shareholders pay tax only on their own earnings.

Closing down

Sole traders and partners can simply close the doors on the business but unless they sell out completely – and selling the business can be a complicated matter – the ghost of business failure can follow them into the bankruptcy court.

It is easier to buy and sell shares in your company. If the company is insolvent, business assets must be liquidated to meet creditors' claims, although they have no claim on the directors' personal assets unless fraud is proved.

Quick comparisons

Although there are legal restrictions on companies, the difference between trading as a sole trader, a partnership or a company is often only one of machinery.

Some concessions have been made to the small company but corporate life remains expensive and time must be spent ensuring that business is carried on in compliance with the Companies Acts. Sole traders and partners lead less complicated legal lives and can generally choose their own route to success or failure. Conversely, unless you have attached restricted voting rights to shares, a bare majority of your company's shareholders can dictate policy, appoint and set directors' salaries, declare dividends and, subject to rather unclear limitations, ratify the acts of directors. Tax is no longer charged at a lower rate on profits retained in the company than the rate charged on the business income of sole traders and partners, regardless of what they drew in cash, and even limited liability is illusory if you are called upon personally to guarantee corporate debts.

Statutory references

Companies Act 1985
European Communities Act 1972
Finance Acts 1965 to 1995
Income and Corporation Taxes Act 1970 (as amended)
Income and Corporation Taxes Act 1988
Limited Liability Partnership Act 2000
Limited Partnership Act 1907
Partnership Act 1890
Single Market Act 1987

2

Getting going

The sole trader for the most part goes his own way. If you take on partners, disagreement between the partners can force a winding up of the business and you need the protection of ground rules set out in a partnership agreement. As director of a limited company you may be even more restricted because you must comply with the Companies Acts.

Business names

Sole traders and *partners* can trade in their own names or under an additional name indicating they have taken over an existing business. Any other name must be registered with the Registrar of Companies. Almost any name is acceptable unless it is misleading and Notes for Guidance are obtainable from Companies House.

Limited partnerships and *limited liability partnerships* must file the partnership name with the Registrar of Companies. The name must not 'offend' the Secretary of State or be a name the use of which would constitute a criminal offence. Again, suitable names are set out in the Notes for Guidance available from Companies House.

Unless you trade in your own name, the business name and your name must be on all business documents with an address at which service of documents concerning the business is accepted. The business name must also be displayed prominently at business premises. Anyone who does business with you but does not visit the premises must be notified in writing of the business name and address.

Companies can use business names showing a continuing connection with the previous proprietor's business.

Companies

A brand-new company's name costs £20 on application for incorporation. Changing the name costs £10.

The last word of the name must be 'limited', or 'cyfyngedig' if the registered office is in Wales. The name must not be 'offensive' to the Secretary of State or one which, if used, would constitute a criminal offence or be the same or similar to that of an existing company.

The Registrar's Index of Company Names should be checked but it does not show pending applications. You may therefore have to make a change within 12 months of registration if the name is the same or 'too like' an existing company name. If the Secretary of State feels misleading information was given or undertakings and assurances given on registration are not met, he has five years during which he can direct that a change be made.

The Registrar reserves the name pending the passing of a special resolution of 75 per cent of the shareholders, a copy of which must be sent to the Registrar with the registration fee. The name cannot be used until you receive the Registrar's certificate and permission may be withdrawn before issue.

Directors are personally liable on contracts made before issue of the certificate and breach of the regulations applying to business and corporate names is a criminal offence.

The company name, registered number, registered office address and the names of the directors must be on all company documents and be prominently displayed at your main business premises.

Domain names

You should also register a domain name on the Internet (see page 123).

Trade marks

Trade marks must be separately registered with the Trade Mark Registry (see Chapter 11).

The partnership agreement

You should have a formal agreement executed in a deed (that is, signed and witnessed) to include:

- **The partnership name and address and the nature of the business.** Business is usually done in the partnership name but implicitly entered into by all the partners, so they are directly liable for business activities. Partnership assets should be put in the partnership's name, or in the name of a maximum of four partners as trustees for the business, to differentiate business assets from personal assets.
- **The date you start and end the partnership.** Fixed period partnerships continue unchanged after the stated date but a single business project partnership ends when the project is completed. If no fixed period or specific business venture is agreed, the partnership ends when a partner gives notice. It is best therefore to state that the partnership can only be terminated by mutual agreement.
- **The amount of capital contributions.** No interest is payable on initial contributions, investments and advances unless stated in the agreement. You should specify whether interest is to be paid on initial contributions before profits are calculated.
- **The bank account.** A statement of who can sign cheques and a provision that payments received for the business are paid into the partnership account.
- **How profits are to be calculated and divided.** In the absence of this clause the partners are entitled to equal shares of cash received, less cash paid, without consideration of book and bad debts, whatever they initially put into the business. It is also advisable to include:

- the spheres of activity of each partner
- whether part-time partners are to draw salaries instead of sharing profits
- a provision that drawings can be made against future profits
- what items, such as cars, not exclusively used for business, can be charged to expenses.

You may also want to specify a top limit on expenses and a figure above which no partner can enter into transactions without the other partners' consent.

- **Accounts.** A provision requiring regular accounts and an annual balance sheet showing what is due to the partners in respect of capital, share of profits and salary.
- **An arbitration clause.** In order that disputes can be referred to an uninvolved outsider to avoid litigation.
- A clause permiting arrangements to be made with creditors through the courts if there are cash flow problems (see page 144).
- **Dissolution.** Failing agreement to the contrary, the partnership is automatically dissolved on a partner's retirement, death or bankruptcy. You should therefore specify how retiring and deceased partners' shares are to be valued and paid off. Alternatively, you can agree to pay an annuity out of profits.

The agreement is binding and can only be altered with the consent of all the partners. *But* it is a private document recording agreement between the partners. For outsiders, if you are a partner with your name on the letterhead, you are responsible for the firm's actions, debts and liabilities unless outsiders are told you are not.

Points 2 and 9 above are important because, for some partnerships a change of partners is a discontinuance of the old partnership and a commencement of a new one for tax purposes. Discontinuance technically dissolves the partnership and the business is taxed as if you had stopped trading and begun again. Each partner is assessed on, and is solely responsible for, the tax on his or her share of partnership profits.

The company's constitution

The *Memorandum of Association* sets out the company's basic constitution and its powers and duties as a legal person. Standard forms are available from The Stationery Office and Companies House, which can be tailored for your purposes before you apply for registration.

The Memorandum must state:

- the company's name which, if you are trading for profit, must include the word 'limited', or, if you are trading in Wales, the Welsh equivalent;
- that the registered office is in England, Wales or Scotland to establish domicile for tax purposes (names of some major cities are also acceptable);
- the objects for which the company is formed, that is a description of the company's objectives and powers and the field in which it does business. Transactions outside or not incidental or ancillary to the company's powers may be void as against the company, although valid and enforceable against management;
- that the liability of shareholders is limited by (their) shares;
- the amount of initial nominal (or authorised) capital and how it is divided into shares (which fixes the fee payable on incorporation). The percentage which is subscribed in cash or asset value is the *issued capital*. Any unpaid balance is *uncalled capital* and shareholders' liability is limited to this amount if the company goes into liquidation;
- the names of subscribers (signatories) to the Memorandum and that they agree to take out at least one share each.

The *Articles of Association* deal with internal organisation, the company's relationship with shareholders and their relationship with each other, the issue of share capital, the appointment and powers of directors and proceedings at meetings. Again, a standard form of Articles is available from The Stationery Office and Companies House.

Registration

On registration you are sent copies of your company's Memorandum and Articles of Association, share transfer forms, a Minute Book, and the Certificate of Incorporation.

First business contracts

Organising the business prior to transferring it to a partnership or limited company transforms you into a promoter. The partnership and company must therefore consent to any profit you make from the sale of assets to them and full details of the transaction must be disclosed.

Selling to the partnership

When you sell to the partnership, the law assumes you act in good faith. You must therefore give your partners full details of any transactions you enter into that affect the partnership, both before and after its formation. The partners can make any arrangement concerning assets which remain the property of individual partners, but once it is agreed that an asset is to belong to the partnership, any increase or reduction in value belongs to the partnership.

Selling to the company

Promoters are personally liable in any transaction made on behalf of the company before incorporation unless there is specific agreement to the contrary. Promoters should therefore contract on the basis that they are no longer liable once the contract is put before the company's board of directors or the general meeting of shareholders, whether or not the company adopts the transaction. Once adopted, the preliminary contract is replaced by a draft agreement which is executed by the company on incorporation.

   Alternatively, you can now enter into a contract for the benefit of your not-yet-incorporated company, provided that the company is specifically identified in the contract by name or description. On incorporation, the company will have the same rights and remedies under the contract as if it had been a party to the contract.

Statutory references

Arbitration Acts 1950, 1975 and 1979
Business Names Act 1985
Companies Act 1975
Contracts (Rights of Third Parties) Act 1999
European Communities Act 1972
Income and Corporation Taxes Act 1970 (as amended)
Limited Liability Partnership Act 2000
Limited Partnership Act 1907
Partnership Act 1890
Registration of Business Names Act 1916

3 *Money*

What you put in the business and what you take out are basic. The sole trader's and partner's freedom to choose their route to profit is counterbalanced by their exposure to personal unlimited liability for business debts, but the directors and management of limited companies are to a large extent protected by the companies legislation.

Sole trader

Business capital is the cash and assets which you put into the business and extra capital can only be raised by way of a loan. Financial commitment is total and takings should not be seen as personal income but as interest-free working and growth capital for the business.

Partnership

Partners are in a similar situation to sole traders but the partners can agree that interest is paid on loans to the business. Failing agreement, there is a 5 per cent limit on advances exceeding initial contributions, unless a different rate can be implied from the custom of the trade or the course of dealing between the partners.

The partnership agreement should therefore specify an annual rate of interest payable on capital from time to time standing to the partners' credit. The amount should be stated to be an outgoing, and deducted and paid as a business expense before profits and profit shares are calculated.

Loans of more than £15,000 including the cost of the credit must comply with the Consumer Credit Act 1974 (see Chapter 9).

You can raise outside capital by taking in a limited partner, whose liability is limited to the amount of the loan. No control is lost because involvement in the business imposes full liability on the limited partner.

Depending on your asset position and profit record additional capital can also be raised at interest and/or on security.

One partner's signature is acceptable in most transactions but your agreement should specify the amount and the kind of transaction which partners can complete on behalf of the business. Loans secured by a charge or mortgage should be approved by all the partners.

Partnership profits

Unless specified in the agreement:

- profits less expenses are business receipts without taking into account work in progress, stock in trade and book debts;
- profits are divided equally;
- partners cannot draw for current expenses against future profits;
- increases in goodwill are not taken into account.

The agreement should therefore make appropriate provision for the above in the annual accounts.

Corporate capital

A company's capital structure is more complicated. If two directors each contribute £300 to form a company with a nominal or authorised capital of £1,000, each taking £50 shares with a par (or nominal) value of £10 per share, or the sole director of a single-member company puts up £600, taking up 100 shares with a par value of £10 per share, the £600 is the company's *paid-up capital*. The £1,000 is the *nominal capital*, that is, the maximum share capital which the Memorandum authorises the company to issue. The balance of £400 is *uncalled capital*. The company can call on this at any time, in accordance with the Articles, unless it is agreed to make all or part *reserve capital* which is only called on in a liquidation.

References to share capital on letterheads and documents must be to paid-up capital. This fixes the minimum value of the net assets which must be raised initially and as far as possible maintained in the business, but usually has no relationship to the value of company assets or the market value of the shares. To see if a company is undercapitalised you must look at the balance sheet.

Corporate profits

Payment for shares can be in cash or in kind, including goodwill, know-how or an undertaking for work or services. The contribution of capital gives a right to a share of distributed profits but does not necessarily fix the proportion to which the contributor is entitled.

Rights attached to shares, including the right to vote and receive dividends, depend on the Memorandum and Articles. Control is retained if you hold 75 per cent of the voting shares.

Most rights can be varied with the consent of three-quarters of the shareholders affected, by their extraordinary resolution or in accordance with a clause in the Memorandum or Articles. Thereafter, changes can only be made by consent and class rights stated to be unalterable in the Memorandum can only be varied with the consent of all the shareholders or by a scheme of arrangement.

Preference shares have a preference over other shares in repayment of capital and/or dividends which are paid at a fixed percentage rate before ordinary dividends. Unless otherwise stated, dividends are cumulative. Arrears must therefore be paid before ordinary dividends but non-cumulative dividends are lost if not paid when due.

Redeemable preference shares are more like debentures which are dealt with below.

Share warrants, with or without voting rights, are usually issued only to fully paid-up shareholders although they are sometimes attached to debentures with an option for future conversion to fully paid-up shares. They are negotiable and, if lost, the holder may lose dividends which are usually paid when the coupon attached to the warrant is sent to the company.

Increasing the company's capital

Increases in capital permitted by the Memorandum must also comply with the Articles but both Memorandum and Articles can, if necessary, be changed to permit an increase.

The Registrar must be notified of increases in capital within 15 days of the passing of the enabling resolution, sent a copy of the minutes of the meeting and, if changed, copies of the amended Memorandum and/or Article.

Shareholders have pre-emptive rights to new issues in proportion to existing holdings, unless this is excluded by the Articles, payment is not in cash, there is a fixed dividend or the directors are authorised to allot shares.

The directors' conditional or unconditional authority to allot shares for a fixed or indefinite period must be included in the Articles or granted by shareholders, who can revoke or vary the authority. If for a fixed period, the expiry date must be stated.

Variation of existing shareholders' rights should be through a scheme of arrangement agreed by a majority of shareholders in number, holding at least three-quarters of the shares. The scheme must be approved by the court.

Shares cannot be issued at less than par value. If new shares are issued at over par value, the premium must be transferred to a share premium account. This is part of the company's capital and can only be distributed with the consent of the court unless used for a bonus or rights issue, as a premium for redemption of redeemable preference shares or debentures, or to write off the expense of another issue.

Reducing the company's capital

The company can reduce its capital by buying back shares. Transactions in small family-run companies are treated as straightforward sales of shares. The only tax payable is capital gains tax but there are heavy penalties if you make mistakes and expert advice should be sought before taking action.

Loans from the company

Special provisions apply to loans and lending facilities extended to directors and their 'connections', and loans and credit facilities of under £15,000, including the cost of the credit, must comply with the Consumer Credit Act 1974.

Loans, guarantees and security of up to £5,000 can be extended to directors and connected persons.

Connected persons are: a director's (business) partner, spouse, child and step-child, companies with which the director is associated and of which he or she controls at least a fifth of the votes at general meetings, a trustee of any trust of which he or she, the family group or associated company is a beneficiary, and the business partner of a connected person.

An advance of up to £10,000 can be made to directors for properly incurred business expenses.

Unlimited loans can be made to directors if made in the ordinary course of business and available on the same terms to outsiders, or the company is in the lending field. Unlimited loans can also be made to directors to enable them properly to perform their duties, provided the shareholders have given their consent, or they approve the loan at the next annual general meeting, or the loan is paid back within six months of the annual general meeting.

Money-lending companies which ordinarily provide such loans to employees can lend up to £100,000 to directors to buy or improve their only or main residence for tax purposes. This is, however, a maximum from which must be deducted other cash or credit facilities already provided. Such companies can also make loans or quasi-loans (undertakings to reimburse a creditor) and extend guarantees to directors and connected persons if they provide the same facilities to outsiders.

Non-cash assets valued at £1,000 or equal to the company's called-up capital cannot be handed to directors, shadow directors or their connections, or acquired by the company without the shareholders' consent either before, or within a reasonable period after, the transaction. If annual accounts comply with the Companies Act, the limit is £50,000 or 10 per cent of the company's net assets as stated in the most recent accounts.

Credit facilities and arrangements and the provision of guarantees and security to directors and their connections must be disclosed in the annual accounts, unless the company's contingent net liability does not exceed £5,000. Other transactions with directors and their connections must be included unless the net value does not exceed £1,000 or 1 per cent of the net value of the company's assets to a maximum of £5,000.

There is no top limit on loans to employees to buy company shares or to set up a trust to buy shares for employees, including full-time salaried directors.

The company can assist anyone to buy its shares, provided its assets are not thereby reduced or, if reduced, the loan comes from distributable profits. The assistance can be by way of gift, loan, guarantee, security, indemnity or any other financial help and must be given in good faith and in the company's interests and with the shareholders' consent. The directors must also make a statutory declaration setting out details of the transaction and their opinion as to the financial viability of the company and the auditors must state whether the directors' opinion is reasonable.

Fines and penalties

Transactions made in contravention of the legislation may be cancelled and repayment or restitution ordered by the court.

Dividends

Dividends must come from profits, not capital. Profits mean accumulated realised profits after account has been taken of depreciation, not previously used for distribution or capitalisation, from which is deducted accumulated realised losses not previously written off.

Dividend declarations are self-contained, so previous losses need not be set against profits and losses, nor do losses on fixed capital have to be made good before profits are ascertained, but you must make up losses of circulating capital.

Loans to the company

Trading companies can borrow and give security without specific provision in the Memorandum and Articles but the Memorandum and Articles should give the company the widest possible powers.

Additional capital can be raised by issuing debentures. These can be in a series with similar rights attached or one of a class when the debenture can be transferable or negotiable.

Debentures secured on specific assets are fixed charges. Charges over all the company's assets, including stock in trade, goodwill and so on, are floating charges. This type of charge permits free dealing with business assets but the charge automatically becomes fixed if the company is wound up or stops trading, or is in default of the terms of the loan and the debenture-holder proceeds to enforce the security. Separate fixed and floating charges can be created but the floating charge is always enforceable after the fixed charge, whenever made, unless the fixed charge prohibits a loan with prior rights and the lender under the fixed charge knows of the restriction. The 1989 Companies Act lists the kind of charges which must be registered at Companies House and the Registrar must be notified of repayment. If not registered, debts are valid but only as unsecured debts. Fixed charges on registered land must also be registered under the Land Registration Act 1925 and on unregistered land under the Charges Act 1972.

The company must keep its own register of charges at the registered office which must be available for public inspection. Copies of the charges must also be available at the registered office for inspection by creditors and shareholders.

If the company is jointly liable with an individual and the loan falls within the Consumer Credit Act 1974, the loan must comply with the Act.

Statutory references

Companies Acts 1985 and 1989
Consumer Credit Act 1974
Finance Act 1982

Income and Corporation Taxes Act 1970 (as amended)
Insolvency Act (No 2) 1994
Land Charges Act 1972
Land Registration Act 1925
Limited Liability Act 2000
Limited Partnership Act 1907
Partnership Act 1890

4 *Running the business*

Sole traders are restricted only by access to capital and their ability to generate profits. Partners and directors share the load but their agreement and cooperation is vital to business success and you may be liable for their incompetence or dishonesty.

Partners' responsibilities

Partners act on behalf of the partnership and their partners. The law implies that they deal with one another fairly and in good faith.

You must therefore account to the business for profits and monies made on business assets and you are liable for any shortfall in payments made by other partners unless the transaction is their personal responsibility. Whatever the partnership agreement states, outsiders can assume partners act for the partnership unless they are informed to the contrary or the transaction is outside the partnership's usual business.

If you do not make specific provision in the agreement the following applies.

- All partners in a trading business can borrow on security and draw, sign, accept and negotiate negotiable instruments; in any other business, they can only draw and endorse ordinary cheques.
- All partners take part in management. If they do not work full time in the business, the partnership can be dissolved – the agreement

could permit partners to go into business on their own account, provided they are not in competition with the partnership.

- Decisions are by partners' majority vote – the agreement could therefore have an arbitration clause so decisions can go to arbitration rather than the courts.
- Profits and losses are divided equally – the agreement should therefore make provision for sharing profits, and paying salaries and interest on capital contributions.
- The agreement should state whether business assets are owned wholly or partly by a partner or the partnership. If the partnership is a partner's tenant and this is not in the agreement, the partnership can only be evicted if the partnership is dissolved. Assets acquired after you start trading belong to the partnership if purchased for business use or on its account but land is a special case. It is classified as 'personal property', not real estate; thus it is considered as a cash sum and must be sold if a partner dies or the partnership is dissolved.

The members (partners) of limited liability partnerships (LLPs) must sign and file the partnership's annual accounts at Companies House and notify it of changes in membership, changes in members' names and addresses, and any change to the Registered Office address.

Third parties will usually contract directly with the LLP which, like a company, is a separate legal entity. The partners are therefore protected by limited liability although individual partners are liable for fraud and may be liable in negligence.

Directors' responsibilities

Whatever the title, a director is anyone occupying the position of a director and anyone in accordance with whose directions the directors are accustomed to act – other than professional advisers. Directors are bound by the powers given by the Memorandum and Articles and their responsibility is to the company, not individual shareholders. They must act honestly and in the company's best interests.

Directors are not responsible for their co-directors' dishonesty. They and management are, however, personally liable to outsiders, the company and shareholders for dishonesty and negligence and for anything done without reference to the company – for instance, placing orders without referring to the company or paying by cheque not properly made out in the company's name. They are also liable for acts done outside the powers set out in the Memorandum and Articles but they are only liable to outsiders if the outsider dealt with them in good faith and the shareholders have not ratified the transaction. If the shareholders refuse approval, the company can also demand reimbursement.

Executive and non-executive directors have the same liability, but only if they are negligent or dishonest and intend to act fraudulently is there a liability for consequential loss caused to the company. Active involvement in a company carrying on business for a fraudulent purpose and continuing to trade when there is no reasonable prospect of creditors being paid can bring a personal liability without limit for all the company's debts and, in addition, a fine and/or imprisonment.

The directors and the company have responsibilities under the employment, industrial training and health and safety legislation and they can be convicted of crimes – for instance, offences under the Road Traffic Acts. The directors are also liable for deficits in the employer's slice of employees' National Insurance contributions and VAT. Directors are required to take note of employees' as well as shareholders' interests but they must also have regard to the best interests of the company.

Directors' service contracts for over 12 months must be available for shareholders' inspection at the registered office or principal place of business. Contracts exceeding five years must be approved by shareholders and if there is no written contract the company must record a memorandum or note of the agreed terms. If you have not changed the standard Articles or there is no special provision in the service contract, a director can be removed from office by shareholders' majority vote and entitlement to compensation depends on the contract. Directors must give written notice of resignation and appointments of successors must be confirmed by the shareholders. The Articles usually provide for a third of the directors to retire each year in rotation but they can be immediately re-elected and a managing director can only be appointed if permitted by the Articles.

Directors and their families cannot buy options on company shares or debentures, although they can receive them as gifts. Details of directors' share and debenture dealings must be given to the company within five days of the transaction.

The Registrar must be kept informed of the names of the directors and where contracts, memoranda and copies are kept.

The company secretary

The company must have a company secretary who can also be a director – although not the sole director – but who cannot then sign documents in both capacities. The secretary's liability is similar to a director's but involvement is often confined to administration, including ensuring documents and returns are sent to the Registrar and that proper company registers are kept. The secretary cannot therefore commit the company in business transactions.

Single-member companies

The single-shareholder company must also have at least one director and a secretary who cannot be the sole director. The single shareholder, in person or by proxy, is a quorum for meetings whatever is stated in the Articles and 'meetings' must be minuted and decisions formally notified to the company, unless made by written resolution.

Details of unwritten contracts between the company and the single shareholder/director must be set out in a memorandum or recorded in the minutes of the next directors' meeting, unless the contract is made in the ordinary course of the company's business.

Auditors

The company must appoint and re-appoint auditors at the annual general meeting, unless the requirement has been dispensed with (see page 31). They are then appointed at least 28 days before the day on which copies of the previous year's accounts are circulated, unless they have been required to put them before the general meeting.

Accounts

The only purpose of accounts for the *sole trader* and *partnership* is to record receipts and payments and chart business progress. Annual accounts are then drawn up showing assets and liabilities and, for the partnership, what is due to each partner. Partners must have access to the books but they are not available to anyone else except the inspector of taxes and the VAT inspector.

Businesses with a turnover of under £15,000 can submit simplified three-line accounts to the Revenue showing only annual turnover, total purchases, expenses and the resulting net profit.

It is proposed to replace abbreviated accounts with 'short-form accounts' for small companies. This is a shortened form of the full accounts that can be filed with Companies House and distributed to shareholders. Instead of a profit-and-loss account, you will be able to set out categories: cost of sales, gross profit, selling and distribution costs, administrative expenses, operating costs and aggregate directors' remuneration. Details of changes in the requirements for the balance sheet are still being discussed. The Directors' Report will be replaced with a 'cover sheet' setting out the names of the directors and secretary, the registered office address and registered number, together with details of, and significant changes in, the company's principal activity.

Company records must comply with the Companies Acts and be more specific. They must explain transactions and disclose the company's financial position with reasonable accuracy so that the directors can ensure the accounts comply with the Acts. Daily receipts and expenses, sales and purchases and details of stock, assets and liabilities must be recorded. Records must be kept for three years and the books must be available to the directors at the registered office or other place designated by the directors.

The accounting reference period (ARP) – the date for the company's financial year – is fixed according to the company's accounting reference date (ARD). The first ARP must be between six and 18 months, beginning with the date of incorporation. Subsequent ARPs are for 12 months. The ARD is fixed at any time within nine months of incorporation by notice given to the Registrar. If none is fixed the ARD is the last day of the month in which the anniversary of incorporation falls.

Copies of the accounts – that is, the balance sheet, profit and loss account, auditor's report and directors' report – must, unless the company has elected to dispense with the requirement, be put before shareholders within ten months of the end of the ARP. Twenty-one days before the meeting copies must be sent to share and debenture holders and to anyone entitled to receive notice of the meeting as well as to the Registrar. Share and debenture holders are entitled also to receive copies of the last accounts.

The directors are responsible for preparing annual accounts and for filing them with the Registrar within the required time limits. They are liable to fines and/or imprisonment for accounts which do not comply with the Acts and late filing. Persistent offenders may be liable to disqualification from acting as a director for up to 15 years.

Exemption from audit for small companies

If turnover is less than £1 million and the balance sheet total does not exceed £1.4 million you can file unaudited accounts. Only an abbreviated balance sheet with explanatory notes must be filed but shareholders must receive the profit and loss account and the directors' report.

The balance sheet must include a statement by the directors that:

- the company was entitled to the exemption;
- shareholders have not demanded an audit;
- they acknowledge responsibility for ensuring the company keeps accounting records in compliance with the Companies Act 1985 and for preparing accounts giving a true and fair view of the company's affairs;
- advantage has been taken of the exemption for individual accounts;
- in their opinion the company is entitled to take advantage of the exemption.

The Articles must permit use of the exemption but shareholders with at least 10 per cent of the company's issued capital or of any class of shares can demand an audit on at least a month's notice to the company's registered office given before the end of the financial year.

The audit exemption for earlier years can be claimed if the accounts are approved by the board and delivered on time but they must then be accompanied by an auditor's report.

If turnover is between £90,000 and £350,000, you must also file an accountant's report, stating whether the accounts agree with the company's records, whether they comply with the Companies Acts and whether the company is entitled to the exemption from audit.

The 'exemption for individual accounts'

Companies with a turnover which does not exceed £2.8 million and/or whose balance sheet total is not more than £1.4 million and/or which employ fewer than 51 people may file abbreviated accounts. Two out of three of the criteria categorise the company. Abbreviated accounts include a short version of the balance sheet with aggregated amounts for each item except debtors and creditors. The directors must file a statement saying they have relied on the exemption because the company is entitled to benefit from it. Full accounts must go to share- and debenture-holders and the report given by the auditors to the annual general meeting must be filed endorsed with a note stating that in their opinion the requirements for the exemption are satisfied.

Keeping the shareholders informed

The report, which must be signed by a director or the company secretary, must give a 'fair review of the development of the business... during the year and the position at the end of it' and include everything which materially affects the company, including details of:

- dividends, what is to be carried to reserve and retained for investment and bad debts;
- directors and their share- and debenture-holdings unless included in the notes to the accounts;
- directors' acquisition of company shares verified by the auditors;
- indemnities covering company officers;

- new share and debenture issues;
- the company's main activity and material changes in the company's business and asset position;
- important events affecting the company during the year, likely future developments and an outline of research and development activities;
- political and charitable gifts exceeding £200.

Shareholders' meetings

Unless you have elected to dispense with meetings, there must be an annual general meeting within 18 months of incorporation and once every subsequent calendar year.

The annual general meeting considers the accounts and reports, approves dividends, elects directors and appoints, re-appoints and agrees auditors' fees. Given the necessary majority of shareholders, the company can be forced to present a resolution for discussion at the annual general meeting. Otherwise, the directors or, depending on the Articles, two or more holders of more than a tenth of the fully paid-up voting shares can call an extraordinary general meeting to deal with other company business.

The auditors and shareholders must be notified of meetings and what is to be discussed in compliance with the Articles. Shareholders can speak and vote through a proxy. Notice is given when posted but the Articles should state that non-receipt will not invalidate meetings. Ninety-five per cent of the holders of voting shares can agree to dispense with notice and can agree not to meet at all, but dispensing with notice of the annual general meeting requires the consent of all shareholders with voting rights.

Resolutions are ordinary, special or extraordinary, depending on what is discussed. Ordinary and special resolutions are passed by a majority of those at the meeting and extraordinary resolutions need a three-quarters majority. Decisions are put to meetings by resolution and when passed bind the directors. Broadly, shareholders acting together can do anything permitted by the company's Memorandum and Articles unless it is prohibited by the Companies Acts, outsiders or creditors are affected or there is a public interest issue.

As an alternative and in spite of anything stated in the Memorandum and Articles, decisions can be made by written resolution, signed by all the shareholders entitled to vote, without serving notice of the contents and calling a meeting. The resolution must be minuted and the auditors must receive copies; the decision is only valid if they do not respond within seven days or they state it does not affect them as auditors or, if so, it does not require discussion at a shareholders' meeting.

This procedure enables the company, with the shareholders' consent, to dispense with some statutory requirements including having an annual general meeting, laying accounts before shareholders, voting to appoint auditors and extending the directors' indefinite authority (that is, beyond the five-year limit) to allot shares. Consent to the procedure must be obtained of all the shareholders.

Anyone can chair meetings but the chairman of the board, if any, usually does so. Company business is, however, usually decided at board meetings and the board's powers depend on the Articles. Board meetings can be held anywhere and at any time but shareholders must be kept informed.

Minutes of meetings must be recorded in a Minute Book kept at the registered office and procedural points not included in, or prohibited by, the Memorandum and Articles can be written into the minutes. The decision who is to sign company cheques should be minuted unless the form of draft resolution sent by the company's bank is passed.

If management acts in good faith and in the company's interests, minority shareholders cannot interfere in the business. Shareholders can sue the company in their own name to protect individual rights but not to protect the company's interests, nor can they interfere with internal management. Otherwise only the company acting in general meeting can take legal action and the will of majority shareholders is therefore the will of the company. Shareholders, directors, personal representatives and liquidators can stop management acting illegally or beyond the powers given in the Memorandum and Articles or if the company's affairs are being conducted in a way which is, or will be, unfairly prejudicial to their interests. However, unless there is fraud or an unfair manipulation of the advantages of a majority holding or management is grossly negligent, the Memorandum and Articles can provide for ratification of almost anything by special or ordinary resolution.

A founding shareholder, one who has held shares for six months or has inherited the shares of a deceased shareholder can ask the court to wind up the company on the ground that it is 'just and equitable' to do so. The order will only be made if there is no other remedy and the shareholder is not being unreasonable in insisting on a winding up.

As a last resort and only on substantial grounds, the Department of Trade and Industry can be called in to investigate the company but the complaining shareholders must lodge security for the costs of the investigation.

Statutory references

Business Names Act 1985
Civil Liability (Contribution) Act 1978
Companies Acts 1985 and 1989
Company Directors Disqualification Act 1986
Industrial Training Act 1982
Insolvency Act 1986
Limited Liability Partnership Act 2000
Limited Partnership Act 1890
Registration of Business Names Act 1916
Road Traffic Act 1972
Transport Act 1968

5

Premises

You should seek legal and financial advice before investing in business premises and rent, which can be a substantial investment and a major part of your overheads.

Planning permission

Check whether current, proposed use or alterations are permitted by the local authority and/or local by-laws and if there have been complaints about use of the premises.

If you need consents it is worth making preliminary investigations yourself. You should also check whether you need anyone else's agreement including someone with an interest in the premises, such as the freeholder and lessees with tenancies with at least ten years to run.

Some building does not require planning permission, including, subject to conditions, a 10 per cent addition to cubic content – not square footage. Some changes of use are also permitted, for instance from one shop to another. You need consent for 'material' change, demolition, most building works and 'material' widening of access to the highway, and sometimes for outside advertisements.

If the vendor has outline permission, check that time limits have not been exceeded – full, as opposed to outline, permission normally lasts for five years.

Unauthorised continuous use since the end of 1963 can be regularised with an established use certificate, otherwise it is unlawful. The occupier is liable for unlawful use and a vendor's undertaking, and indemnity for damages is no protection. Suing for misrepresentation and/or breach of covenant in a lease is expensive and of little value compared with the expense and impact of eviction without notice.

Leases

The landlord may have to consent to sale, alteration and/or change of use under an existing lease. Consent must be given within a reasonable time unless it is reasonable to withhold it and the landlord must serve written notice of the decision, specifying any conditions attached to the consent or the reasons for withholding it.

The landlord may have to consent to sale, alterations and/or change of use under an existing lease. Payment cannot be demanded from the incoming tenant, and if there are no structural alterations, the rent should not increase even if permitted by the lease. But the incoming tenant may have to undertake to reinstate premises if this is reasonable and pay for damage or diminution in value to the property or the landlord's adjoining property, as well as legal and other expenses.

The lease can prohibit change of use, alterations and improvements and the landlord can refuse consent unless the lease states consent cannot be 'unreasonably withheld'. Reasonable reasons must be given by the landlord; requiring more than the cost of actual compensation constitutes unreasonable refusal. The landlord cannot unreasonably withhold consent or impose unreasonable conditions if you make a written request to make reasonable alteration to the premises to accommodate disabled employees (see page 82).

An incoming tenant should ensure the vendor has a right to sell or sublet. Landlord and tenant can agree when the landlord can refuse to permit a sale of the lease, by for example forbidding a sale in the first or last three years of the term. They can also agree conditions, for example, requiring an incoming tenant to give a bank guarantee. But if the landlord or a third party is unilaterally able to decide when and/or on what conditions you can sell, the terms of the lease must either require the decision to be reasonable or give you the right to have the matter independently decided. If this agreed term in the lease is worded inappropriately the landlord cannot unreasonably withhold consent, whatever the circumstances. If the sale requires the landlord's consent, a suitable tenant must be accepted, unless refusal is reasonable on grounds which would have been valid when the lease was created or it last changed hands. Payment for consent to sale or sublet can be demanded only if permitted by the lease.

If, unknown to the purchaser, the vendor has no right to sell or sublet, the landlord must accept the purchaser and seek compensation from the vendor, but the purchaser may have to vacate if change of use is in breach of a superior lease or planning consent.

If the lease is for a fixed period or from year to year following a lease for a period of months or years, you can usually continue in occupation after expiry of the lease on the same terms. The Landlord and Tenant Act 1954 excludes some tenancies from the protection, including tenants living on the premises (who may be protected under the Rent Acts).

Renewal is subject to negotiation at the end of the tenancy and strict formalities and time limits apply. Usually the landlord must give between 6 and 12 months' notice, setting out the tenant's rights and stating whether he will oppose an application for a new tenancy. Otherwise the existing tenancy continues until the tenant asks for renewal.

The landlord's claim to possession must be on grounds contained in the 1954 Act, which are broadly similar to those in commercial leases, including delay in paying rent and failure to maintain, repair, use or manage the premises. The tenant must move if the landlord offers suitable alternative accommodation, the premises are to be let as part of a larger, more profitable unit or they are to be redeveloped or used by the landlord.

If negotiations break down, you can apply to the county court for a new lease. Again, there are time limits and whatever the stage of negotiations, apply to the court for a new tenancy two to four months after service of the landlord's notice of termination, otherwise you will lose your right to remain in occupation.

If you go to court and the landlord cannot prove one of the statutory grounds, the court must grant a tenancy of up to 14 years on much the same terms as the old one, although rent is based on open market value.

If the only issue is the terms of the new lease, it may be cheaper and faster to use the Royal Institute of Chartered Surveyors (RICS) and Professional Arbitration on Court Terms (PACT) arbitration scheme.

If the landlord proves his case and you must move, you are entitled to *compensation for improvements*, provided you served three months' notice of your intention to do the work and there was no objection. If the landlord objected, you can apply to court for a certificate stating it was reasonable to do the work and again there are time limits.

Continuous occupation for 14 years entitles you to *compensation for disturbance* if the landlord is to let the premises as part of a larger unit or intends to redevelop or use them himself.

Outgoing tenants and their guarantors are now automatically released from the covenants when the lease is sold, but their involvement does not necessarily end. If the lease requires the landlord or anyone else to consent to the sale and also requires the outgoing tenant to guarantee the incoming tenant – under an 'authorised guarantee agreement' – the outgoing tenant or his guarantor can be called upon to remedy the incoming tenant's breach of certain covenants. If the outgoing tenant or guarantor then 'remedies the breach', for example by paying the amount or taking the action demanded by the landlord, either can claim a lease of the premises which overrides the incoming tenant's right to occupy.

NB: These provisions are fenced around with rules and regulations, requiring formal notices to be served on the various parties within specified time limits. Both tenants and landlord should therefore ensure they are fully informed as to the implications of the legislation.

Stamp duty

The proposed new rates and thresholds for stamp duty for 2001/02 are:

Up to £60,000	nil
Over £60,000 up to £250,000	1%
Over £250,000 up to £500,000	3%
Over £500,000	4%

The rate of duty applies to the whole purchase price. The scale also applies to other property transactions, such as goodwill and some forms of debt but not to intellectual property.

Leases

Stamp duty on assignment of an existing lease is charged in the same way as transfer of a freehold. On the grant of a new lease, duty is charged separately on the premium at the same rate as for a sale and on the average annual rent under a scale of rates that varies with the length of the term. The new rates apply to lease premiums in the same way as to sales of freeholds.

There is a separate scale of rates of duty on rent but the threshold for the stamp duty charge on annual rent for new leases of up to seven years or of an indefinite term has been raised to £5,000.

Rent arrears

The landlord can seize the tenant's assets – levy distress – and sell them if rent is in arrear but only:

- if the tenant has a continuing tenancy; or
- if the tenancy has ended, during the six months after expiry;

and then only in daylight hours from Monday to Saturday inclusive. The right to levy distress is subject, and without prejudice, to the rights of prior creditors. If the landlord breaks the rules he is liable to damages.

NB: Landlord and tenant law is a technical area with infinite possibilities for expensive error, and before taking on a lease you should take legal advice.

Conditions of work

The Health and Safety at Work Act 1974 applies to premises where anyone is employed and covers employees, independent contractors, visitors, trespassers and the general public.

The Act is primarily aimed at preventing accidents and imposing fines and penalties and both you and the business can be prosecuted. There is strict (automatic) liability for business activities which affect the health or safety of the public and if there is pollution the local authority can order works to be carried out or close you down. There is no time limit for prosecutions. Serious offences carry unlimited fines and up to two years' imprisonment and there is a continuing daily fine for some offences. It may therefore be helpful to consult the inspectorate and Employment Medical Advisory Service (EMAS) if business activities are likely to cause problems.

Employees must work in reasonable safety and comfort, welfare and catering arrangements and toilet facilities must be clean and safe and you are responsible for clothing left on the premises. Continuing instruction, information, training and supervision must be provided to protect employees' health and safety, particularly if they are inexperienced or have a poor command of English and they must use the protection and information provided.

Employees working with dangerous substances must be monitored and records kept for at least five years. If some dangerous substances are used, the employer must pay for employees to have regular health checks. Similar obligations apply to workers in the electrical industry.

Employers' liability to employees cannot be excluded or restricted for injury caused by defective plant, machinery, equipment or protective clothing and equipment. The liability cannot be delegated, unless it is reasonable to rely on expert advice or information or on the established practice of the trade.

If employees are sent to someone else's premises, your responsibility is reduced to taking 'reasonable' care that they have a safe system of work and usually the responsibility then passes to the owner of the premises. Owners of machinery or equipment left on your premises are liable to anyone using it with their consent.

If you employ more than five people, *health, safety, welfare information and emergency safety procedures* must be displayed on the premises and rules about health and safety with details of management's and employees' responsibilities must be set out in a written statement which must be kept up to date. Employees who belong to a trade union can appoint a safety representative who must be consulted about your procedures and they can ask for a supervisory safety committee to be appointed. Drivers of vehicles carrying dangerous substances must be informed of the hazards involved and of emergency avoidance action. The information must be displayed in the cab of the vehicle.

Codes of practice covering health and safety procedures are available from The Stationery Office. It is a defence to show that you took all reasonable precautions and exercised due diligence. Accordingly, although non-compliance is not an offence, it can be persuasive evidence against you.

If you manufacture, supply or import goods, plant and machinery, systems of work and methods of handling, storage and transport must be safe, suitable and without risk to health.

Manufacturers, suppliers, installers and anyone responsible for maintenance and handling a defective product is liable to you and anyone employed by you or injured on your premises. The employer, however, still has primary responsibility even if an accident is due to someone else's careless or intentional act.

Designers, manufacturers, importers and suppliers of goods are responsible for them, unless the buyer carries out his own safety checks. But, unless you can reasonably rely on someone else's research, you must give proper instructions for use and carry out research to minimise health and safety hazards.

Claims for compensation for personal injury must usually be made within three years of the injury and may be reduced to reflect a claimant's own carelessness. The employer must carry compulsory insurance and a copy of the policy must be displayed on your premises unless you only employ close relatives or independent contractors. Employees can also claim for industrial injury under the Social Security Act 1975, payable by the Department for Work, Family and Pensions.

Employees' responsibilities

Employees must follow reasonable orders and safety regulations and take reasonable care of themselves and anyone else affected by their work. The law assumes they work carefully, competently and reasonably skilfully and take proper care of your property, but if there is an accident you may be liable for employing unsuitable people. Even if you specifically forbid an action, you are usually responsible for damage caused by an employee in the course of his employment, although the employee may be wholly or partly liable for his own deliberate and voluntary act which puts himself and others at risk.

Employer's vicarious liability

You and your business can be convicted for offences committed by an employee which are regarded as your offences – for instance, if your lorry is on the road with an insecure load – and for an employee's negligence or theft on the job. Each offence must be seen in the context of the harm it is designed to avoid and there are some defences but, broadly, the test is would a reasonable man say:

- that the employee's act is part and parcel of the employment, even though unauthorised or prohibited – *vicarious liability and employer liable*; or
- that it is so divergent as to be plainly alien to it – *employee liable*?

In transactions with businesses – but not with consumers – you can exclude civil liability by contract. But it must be reasonable for the risk to fall on the other party and the clause must be clear, unambiguous and brought to the attention of the other party.

Independent contractors and the self-employed

Independent contractors and the self-employed have their own responsibilities. They must not expose co-workers to risk but even if contracts provide for split liability, all the responsibility falls on one party if the other is unable to pay compensation.

Temporary workers

Responsibility for and to temporary workers depends on whether they have a contract of employment or have worked sufficiently long for you to be considered their employer. If engaged through an agency, you are responsible for them only if there is a personal obligation to do the work or the agency is a placement bureau.

Factories

When employees do manual work for pay the premises are transformed into a factory and brought within the ambit of the Factories Act and the employer in 'control' of the premises takes on occupier's liability. Even running a self-service car wash may give sufficient control, although a 'responsible employee' may also wholly or partly share liability.

The Act aims to protect workers in an industrial environment against risks to which they are exposed daily. There must therefore be a safe system of work, the premises and access must, so far as is reasonably practicable, be made and kept safe and potentially dangerous machinery must be fenced. Floors, steps, stairs, passages and gangways must be soundly constructed and maintained and, so far as is reasonably practicable, be free from obstruction and substances likely to cause anyone to slip. Liability here may be shared with independent contractors and you should specifically so provide in your contracts with them.

Health and welfare provisions, similar to those applying to offices and shops, are summarised below and the Health and Safety Executive must be given details about the employer, the business, the work and whether any mechanical power is used. Written notification of accidents causing death, or disablement lasting more than three days which precludes normal work, and of certain specified industrial diseases must also be given.

Offices and shops

Under the Offices, Shops and Railway Premises Act 1963:

- An office is any building solely or principally used as an office or for office purposes and to further such activities, including rooms used as staff canteens and storage.
- A shop is premises used for retail trade; and a shop assistant is anyone wholly or mainly engaged to serve customers, take orders or dispatch goods.
- Trade includes buying, selling, retail sale at auction, lending books for profit, hairdressing, barber shops, the sale of refreshments and intoxicating drinks, buildings where wholesalers keep or dispose of stock or to which the public have access to effect their own repairs, premises used to store and sell fuel and staff canteens.

The prospective occupier must give the local authority two copies of a written notice stating his intention to take over premises at least a month prior to occupation or use and must notify the local authority of accidents and industrial diseases in accordance with the 1974 Act.

Health and welfare provisions

Again, the aim is to protect workers in their everyday working environment. Premises must be kept clean and sanitary and dirt and refuse must be removed daily from the floors. There are detailed provisions for washing walls and ceilings and redecorating. Proper drainage must be provided if necessary to a manufacturing process.

Factories must not be overcrowded and similar provisions apply to the parts of shops and offices which are not open to the public or used for the sale of goods to customers.

Proper and suitable lighting, heating and ventilation must be provided, with sufficient, suitable, clean and properly lit sanitary conveniences. Drinking water must be accessible. First aid supplies must be kept on the premises with a responsible person in charge – a nurse or person qualified in first aid if there are more than 50 employees. Medical supervision may be required if there is a risk of injury to health, new processes or substances are introduced, or young people are employed.

Employer protection

Employers can protect themselves by preparing a safety at work scheme after consultation with employees or their trade union representatives, which should be reviewed annually. Protective clothing and equipment with instructions for use should be provided and employees should be reminded of risks. Emergency and safety procedures and directions for the use of protective clothing and equipment should be displayed on the premises. If use of safety equipment is part of the contract of employment or a provision of works' rules, employees can be fairly dismissed – after due warnings – if they do not observe procedures. You should also have the back-up protection of voluntary and compulsory insurance.

Special legislation for certain trades

Some trades require special licences. You should therefore check with your local authority requirements.

Retail shops

You should check with the local authority to find out if there is any restriction on opening hours.

'Small shops' with a floor area of less than 280 square metres can stay open as long as they like on Sundays to sell:

- their farm produce;
- alcoholic drinks;
- vehicle and motorcycle supplies and accessories;
- pharmaceutical supplies, medicinal products and appliances.

There is also no limit on Sunday trading for:

- small airport and railway shops;
- shops in service areas and filling stations;
- shops at airports and ports selling food and necessaries;
- food-stands at exhibitions.

Statutory references

Arbitration Act 1996
Civil Liability (Contribution) Act 1978
Clean Air Act 1993
Congenital Disabilities Act 1975
Consumer Protection Act 1987
Control of Pollution Act 1974
Employers' Liability (Compulsory Insurance) Act 1969
Employers' Liability (Defective Equipment) Act 1969
Environmental Protection Act 1990
Estate Agency Act 1979

Factories Act 1961
Fatal Accidents Act 1976
Health and Safety at Work Act 1974
Landlord and Tenant Act 1954 (Part II)
Landlord and Tenant Act 1927 & 1988
Landlord and Tenant (Covenants) Act 1995
Latent Damage Act 1986
Law Reform (Contributory Negligence) Act 1945
Law Reform (Miscellaneous Provisions) Act 1934
Limitation Act 1980
Occupiers' Liability Acts 1957 and 1974
Offices, Shops and Railway Premises Act 1963
Race Relations Act 1976
Rent Act 1977
Sex Discrimination Act 1975
Social Security Act 1975
Sunday Trading Act 1994
Town and Country Planning Act 1971
Unfair Contract Terms Act 1977

6 *Tax*

A short guide to tax is included for completeness, but your first and best adviser is your accountant, who has a broad general knowledge and experience of finance and the law. Accountants are, however, general practitioners and you are advised to ask to be referred to a specialist for difficult questions of law.

The tax bill

Tax is paid on business profits, but the calculation and amount depends on whether you are personally assessed for tax – as sole trader, partner or director – or whether the business is taxed separately. Sole traders and partners pay tax on business profits, but the company pays its own tax.

The tax on business profits for sole traders and partners is paid in three instalments:

1. 'Interim payments' – payments on account on 31 January.
2. A payment on 31 July in the year of assessment; these are usually 50 per cent of the preceding year of assessment's income tax liability, less tax deducted at source.
3. A payment on 31 January following the end of the year of assessment. This comprises the balance of income tax due plus capital gains tax.

No interim payments are due in the year in which you start business, and if you stop trading or profits fall and you think you are liable to less or no tax, you can make an appropriate claim to the Inland Revenue.

Directors are taxed on their income – that is, salary and dividends. The company pays corporation tax (CT) on profits no later than nine months and one day after the end of the accounting period – that is, on profits for the period for which the company's accounts are drawn up. If you have a close company (see page 7), CT and income tax may also be due on loans to participators and their associates in a close company.

Independent taxation

Married couples are taxed as separate individuals. Income and capital gains are taxed separately. For 2001/02, everyone has a single person's allowance of £4,535. A married couple living together are entitled to married couple's allowance of £536.50 if either was aged 65 or over on 5 April 2000. The amounts are decreased if income exceeds certain limits and are increased for older taxpayers. The married couple's allowance is set against the husband's income. If it is insufficient to cover the allowance, the surplus is transferred to the wife.

Children's tax credit (CTC) is available to couples or single parents with at least one child under the age of 16 living with them for part of the tax year. CTC reduces by £1 for every £15 by which the claimant's taxable income exceeds £29,400. Married couples holding joint assets each bear half the tax, unless they make a declaration stating assets are not owned equally. Both can claim Enterprise Investment Scheme (EIS) relief and their own deductions for trading losses, pension contributions, etc. Chargeable gains are also taxed separately.

Self-assessment

Sole traders, partners and companies now calculate their own tax bill or ask the Inland Revenue to do it for them.

Self-assessment brings heavy responsibilities for the taxpayer. There is an automatic penalty of at least £100 if returns are filed late or rejected.

Interest and a surcharge is charged on tax paid late. The Inland Revenue pays interest at the same rate on overpayment, which is treated as business income and is therefore taxable.

There are fines of up to £3,000 if you cannot produce evidence to support your calculations. All documents relevant to tax affairs should therefore be retained, such as incidental receipts and details of taxable benefits, including tips and expenses. Traders should retain copies of sale and purchase invoices and a daily record of goods taken from stock for private use and goods and services bartered with other traders. If telephones and cars are for both private and business use, itemised bills should be appropriately marked to show which charges relate to the business. The self-employed and companies should retain these records for six years from 31 January following the tax year and employees for about two years, or from the end of the accounting period, and employers for three years. The Inland Revenue can take proceedings up to 21 years after the end of a company's accounting period if there is negligence or fraud and can charge a tax-related penalty of up to a maximum of the understated tax.

Tax and the European Union

Basic elements for the harmonisation of *corporate* tax systems have been agreed, but are not yet implemented.

Business rates

This is a local property tax paid by occupiers of business premises based on rateable value, which is determined by market rents and updated (revalued) every five years. Current business rates came into effect in April 2000 and reflect open-market rents on 1 April 1998. The rating list can be inspected at your local authority offices, the local Valuation Office or at www.voa.gov.uk. If you use part of your home for business, you may be liable for business rates on that part. The extent of business use must, however, be clearly identifiable – for instance, business use of a specific room or a garage. A free leaflet, 'Business Rates Advice', is obtainable from the Royal Institute of Chartered Surveyors. Your local Valuation

Office can advise you on how to appeal if you think you are paying too much.

The sole trader and the partnership

The sole trader and the partners are personally liable for tax on business profits, and retiring partners take their tax liability with them. If they die, it passes to their estates.

Although the partners are separately assessed to income tax, the partnership must send in a Partnership (Tax) Return setting out the partnership's profits or losses and showing how they are divided between the partners.

If annual turnover is less than £15,000, you do not have to provide detailed accounts and information in your tax return, but can instead submit a simple three-line summary.

The sole trader is taxed as if business income is his or her income. Both sole traders and partners are personally liable for tax deducted from employees' pay and partners are personally liable for tax on their share of partnership income, which must be included in their tax return.

For your first year, you pay tax on a current-year basis on profits from your start date to the following April. The second period is generally 12 months ending on a date that is then your usual 'year end' or 'accounting' date.

Some business expenses, such as wages, rent and rates, qualify for tax relief if incurred not more than three years before you start trading.

For 2001/02, sole traders and partners – like employees – pay tax on income less personal tax reliefs at 10 per cent (starting rate) on the first £1,880, at 22 per cent (the basic rate) on the next £27,520 and at 40 per cent (the higher rate) on income over £29,400.

If you hold shares in a company, you pay an additional 10 per cent income tax on dividends of between £26,880 and £28,400 and 32.5 per cent on dividend income exceeding £29,400.

Unlike employees, sole traders and partnerships can deduct from profits day-to-day (revenue) expenses wholly and exclusively incurred in carrying on business. The previous year's losses are also deductible against income. Any balance remaining can be carried forward and set off against future profits or carried back and set off against earlier profits. Losses in the first four years' trading can be set off against earlier income from any other source in the three years before starting the new business, and a limited partner is entitled to tax relief for the full amount of his or her share of the loss, even if it exceeds the original contribution.

Allowable business expenses

The main expenses that can be deducted from profits as revenue expenses are:

- Running costs, including heating, lighting, rent rates, telephone, postage, advertising, special clothing, cleaning and repairs, but *not* improvements (a capital expense). If you live on your business premises, you can claim a proportion, but may then be liable to CGT and business rates.
- Research and development (R&D) costs. As from 12 April 2000 you can claim R&D tax credits if you invest at least £25,000 in the tax year. This allows deduction of 150 per cent (instead of 100 per cent) of qualifying expenditure, plus a cash payment of £24 for every £100 if the company is not making profits. Staff wages and relevant consumables constitute qualifying expenditure, as well as some costs of subcontracting R&D.
- Goods bought for resale and materials for manufacturing, but *not* plant, cars or machinery (capital expenses), although some smaller items may be allowable.
- Carriage, packing and delivery costs.
- Wages, including your spouse's and the directors, but *not* a sole traders or the partners'.
- Interest on business loans and overdrafts, but *not* on partners' advances.
- Charges for hire, hire purchase and leasing, but *not* the cost price (a capital expense).
- Insurance, but *not* NICs or your life insurance.
- Premiums for employees' liability insurance, including directors' and officers' liability and professional indemnity insurance, and payment of work-related uninsured liabilities.

- Subscriptions to professional and trade organisations.
- Expenses of business trips, but *not* travel between home and a fixed place of work.
- Car running expenses, plus the cost of fuel used for business purposes. Up to £5 (£10 when abroad) for employees' personal expenses when away from home on business.
- Other overseas expenses – weekend and overnight conferences – may also be deductible.
- Entertaining your own staff.
- Some professional fees, eg audit fees, legal advice and the cost of legal proceedings relating to the business, but *not* penalties for breaking the law, eg fines.
- Bad debts, but *not* a general provision for a percentage of unspecified bad debts.
- VAT on business expenses, eg petrol, but *not* if you are a taxable trader for VAT purposes.
- Charitable gifts, including gifts of shares to charities.
- Business gifts of up to £50.
- Donations to Learning and Skills Councils.

Companies' allowable expenses against profits are similar to those for the sole trader and partnership, except you can also deduct directors' pay. If there is no dispute, the company can claim repayment of income tax (eg deducted at source on interest received) and tax credits (on UK dividends) before profits are agreed.

Capital allowances

For both income tax and CT, the depreciation to be deducted in the accounts is replaced by capital allowances, which are deducted from the tax bill. The main capital allowances are:

- *private cars*: 25 per cent of the reducing balance to a maximum of £3,000 per car;
- *plant and machinery*: 40 per cent of first-year allowance for the small business;

- *computers*: 100 per cent of first-year allowance for the small business;
- *industrial buildings*: 4 per cent of cost;
- *enterprise zone buildings*: 100 per cent of initial allowance.

Companies must disclaim allowances if they do not wish to use them, but claims can be amended at a later stage.

Rollover relief

This relief allows tax arising on the sale of business assets to be deferred or 'rolled over' if the proceeds are used to acquire another qualifying business asset. The deferred charge is reinstated when the replacement asset is sold.

Stock relief

Stock must be valued at each accounting date. To take account of inflation, the Inland Revenue allows a relief calculated by applying the increase in value (based on the 'All Stocks Index' to March 1984) to the value at the beginning of the period. Special provisions apply to the first period of trading and you can make a partial claim or apply for succession relief.

Benefits in kind

Directors and employees whose annual salary is £8,500 and over (including benefits) have to pay tax on their income, plus the cash equivalent of the benefit.

Company car taxation

Car benefit

You pay tax on private use of a company car, including journeys to and from work. For 2001/02, the benefit is calculated on the percentages of the list price set out in Table 6.1.

Table 6.1 Company car benefit

Taxable benefit	Car under 4 years	Car 4 years or over
Standard taxable benefit	35.00%	26.25%
Business mileage 2,500–17,999 p/a	25.00%	18.75%
Business mileage 18,000 p/a and over	15.00%	11.25%

Second cars are taxed on the standard 35 per cent benefit, with a reduction to 25 per cent if business travel in the second car exceeds 17,999 p/a. The amount is reduced by one-quarter if the car is four years old on 5 April 2002 and by payments received from the employee for private use.

- The list price relates to the date of first registration. There is an upper limit of £80,000.
- The list price is reduced by the employee's capital contribution when the car is first made available, subject to a maximum deduction of £5,000.
- The vehicle's age is determined at the end of the tax year.
- Second cars are taxed on 35 per cent of the price, reduced to 25 per cent if the car is used for at least 18,000 business miles a year.
- Special rules apply to cars at least 15 years old with a market value of at least £15,000.

From 6 February 2002 the existing system is to be abolished and it is proposed that:

- Company cars, including second cars, will be taxed on the basis of carbon dioxide emissions.
- The existing rules for business mileage and cars over four years old will be abolished.
- The tax charge will be linked to the car's exhaust emissions.

- Cars registered before 1 January 1998 will be taxed according to engine size.
- Cars with no approved figure of carbon dioxide emission and no cylinder capacity will be taxed on 35 per cent of the car's price (32 per cent if registered before 1 January 1998), except for cars running solely on electricity, which will be taxed on 15 per cent of the car's price.

Van benefit

If available for private use, including journeys to and from work, the employee pays tax on a standard charge, based on the van's age, of £500 for a van registered after 5 April 1998 and £350 for older vans. This includes free fuel provided by the employer.

The amount is reduced:

- if the van is available for only part of the tax year;
- if it is unavailable for 30 or more consecutive days;
- by the amount of any money the employee pays for private use.

The cash equivalent of free fuel for private motoring is fixed by reference to engine size and is reduced if the vehicle is not available all the year – see Table 6.2.

The benefit is reduced to nil if employees pay for all private fuel.

Table 6.2   Car fuel benefit

	Petrol	**Diesel**
Up to 1,400cc	£1,930	£2,460
1,401–2,000cc	£2,460	£2,460
Over 2,000cc	£3,620	£3,620

Fixed-profit car scheme

You can choose to use this scheme for employees using their own cars for business. The rates for the maximum tax-free mileage allowances under the scheme are shown in Table 6.3.

Table 6.3 Rates for tax-free mileage allowances

| | Engine capacity | | | | |
	Up to 1,000cc	1,001cc to 1,500 cc	1,501cc to 2,000cc	Over 2,000 cc	Alternative average rate
Business mileage					
First 4,000 miles	40p	40p	45p	63p	42.5p
Over 4,000 miles	25p	25p	25p	36p	25p

The scheme does not cover interest paid by an employee on a loan to purchase a car.

As from 6 April 2002, it is proposed the rates change to 40p per mile for the first 10,000 miles and 25p thereafter, regardless of engine capacity.

You should check with your local Inland Revenue office to find out whether NICs are payable on mileage allowances.

VAT scale charge – VAT due per quarter, per car

VAT scale charges are as shown in Table 6.4.

Table 6.4 VAT scale charges

	Petrol	Diesel
Up to 1,400cc	£36.04	£33.51
1,401–2,000cc	£44.72	£33.51
Over 2,000cc	£67.46	£42.59

The Enterprise Investment Scheme (EIS)

The EIS is a form of high-risk, high-return sponsorship where an outsider invests an annual maximum of £150,000 in unquoted company shares to fund a start-up business and retains the shares for three years. The various IT and CGT reliefs include:

- income tax relief of 20 per cent of the investment but dividends are taxable and the relief is clawed back if the shares are sold within three years;
- relief for any allowable losses against income OR chargeable gains;
- loss on disposal of shares is an allowable loss for CGT purposes;
- deferral of CGT on disposal if the gain is reinvested in shares.

No inheritance tax is payable if the shares are held for two years. The scheme covers most businesses but some are excluded, including financial services and overseas companies.

The Venture Capital Trust (VCT) Scheme

VCTs are companies listed on the Stock Exchange that invest in small higher risk unquoted trading companies. The Scheme covers the same businesses as the EIS and the investor can spread the risk over several qualifying companies obtaining:

- income tax relief at 20 per cent on an investment in new ordinary shares with an annual limit of £100,000 – the shares must be retained for at least three years;
- deferral of CGT on disposal if the gain is invested in shares for which IT relief is obtained;
- exemption from CGT on disposal of ordinary shares;
- exemption from IT on ordinary share dividends.

Corporate Venturing Scheme

This is another tax incentive scheme to encourage companies to invest in small higher risk unquoted trading companies enabling the investor company to:

- obtain corporation tax relief at 20 per cent on amounts invested in new ordinary shares held for at least three years;
- defer tax on gains which are reinvested in another shareholding under the scheme;
- claim relief against income for capital losses net of corporation tax relief on disposals of shares.

Some small companies whose income mainly derives from licence fees and royalties are excluded from the Scheme. The corporate investor's maximum stake cannot exceed 30 per cent and individual shareholders in the small company must retain at least 20 per cent of the small companies share capital.

Corporation Tax (CT)

The rates of CT for 2001/02 are shown in Table 6.5.

Table 6.5   Corporation tax rates

Starting rate	10%	on	£0–10,000
Marginal relief		on	£10,000–50,000
Small company rate	20%	on	£50,001–300,000
Marginal relief		on	£300,001–1,500,000
Main rate	30%	on	£1,500,000 plus

Small companies' marginal relief fraction is 1/40

Profits are adjusted by the various allowances and deductions to calculate taxable profit for CT are based on the relevant accounting period. Losses can be carried back against the previous year's profits. A three-year carry-back is available for losses arising in the last 12 months before cessation.

A notice to deliver the Company Tax Return is sent to the company between three and seven weeks after the end of its accounting period, requiring the completed Tax Return for a period of not more than 12 months to be sent to the Revenue by the statutory filing date, ie within three months of receipt of the Notice or 12 months after the end of the accounting period, depending on when the Notice is received and the company's accounting date.

The Tax Return is a self-assessment of the company's tax liability and you must send in accounts drawn up in accordance with the Companies Acts or computations showing how the figures have been arrived at from the figures in the accounts, and the other documents required by the Companies Acts, such as the directors' report, the auditors' report and details of close company's loans to participators and their associates.

Profits are adjusted by the various allowances and deductions to calculate taxable profit for CT based on the relevant accounting period.

Accounting records should be retained for at least six years from the end of the accounting period, either originals or an acceptable alternative form, eg in an optical imaging system or other system which shows you have made a complete and correct Company Tax Return and you must retain original vouchers for tax deducted or tax credits.

Payment is made in a lump sum nine months after the end of the accounting period electronically through BACS and CHAPS or by GIRO or cheque to your company's Inland Revenue Accounts Office at Cumbernauld or Shipley. Interest on late payments is a deductible business cost and interest paid by the Revenue on early payments and over-payments is taxed as income.

The Revenue has at least twelve months to question the assessment. The company is notified of an enquiry and when it finishes and of any adjustments in the tax due.

Contact your local Inland Revenue Enquiry Centre if in doubt as to the deadline for payment or what has to be done.

Inheritance Tax (IT)

No IT is payable for 2001/02 on transfers under £242,000 or any transfer by individuals unless made within seven years of death. Tapering relief applies to transfers made between three and seven years of death. Thereafter the rate is 40 per cent. The amounts to which the varying percentages apply are index-linked to changes in the retail price index.

Capital Gains Tax (CGT)

Capital gains for individuals and companies are taxed as income. Individuals pay at the rate paid on the top slice of income and companies at the CT rate. Disposals for 2001/02 are exempt where the real or notional gain is less than £7,500. The limit is index-linked and gains are reduced by increasing allowable expenditure in accordance with the increase in the index.

Disposal of the business is liable to tax but if you sell and buy another business within three years, you can defer payment until you finally dispose of the new business and stop trading. The relief is particularly helpful if you have been using your home as business premises and claiming tax relief for part of the running expenses.

Disposal of business assets

Tapering relief applies to disposals of business assets after 6 April 2000, including shares held by employees in unquoted companies. See Table 6.6.

Table 6.6 Tapering relief

Period asset held in years	Percentage of gain chargeable	Effective rate for higher-rate CGT taxpayer
0–1	100%	40%
1–2	87.5%	35%
2–3	75%	30%
3–4	50%	20%
4 plus	25%	10%

Value Added Tax (VAT)

As from 1 April 2001 if annual taxable outputs of the business (charges for goods and services) exceed or are likely to exceed £54,000 including VAT, you must register with Customs and Excise for VAT. The limit is based on the past 12 months' turnover and if at the end of a month, taxable supplies in the last 12 months exceed the limit or might do so in the next 30 days, registration is compulsory. You can apply for registration if turnover is below the limit but there is a discretion to refuse it.

If you think your annual turnover will not reach £52,000 excluding VAT, you can apply for cancellation. If you hold less than £5,714 worth of stock and assets you do not have to repay VAT on deregistration.

You can account for VAT based on actual receipts and payments instead of invoice dates if your annual turnover does not exceed £600,000.

If you have not registered for VAT and dispose of capital assets and obtain a VAT refund you may have to pay over the VAT to Customs and Excise.

Invoices must show your VAT-registered number and details of sales including the rate charged and the amount and that they be available for inspection. VAT returns must be completed at the end of the VAT accounting period to show total outputs and the VAT charged. Against this is set total inputs and the VAT paid. If outputs exceed inputs, the balance must be paid to Customs and Excise and if you paid out more than you received, you can claim the difference.

Some businesses are covered by special schemes, there are special rules for discounts, free gifts, samples, hire purchase and 'self-supply' and bad debt relief is available. It is proposed that some property conversion and renovation work will become liable to VAT at 5 per cent instead of the current 17.5 per cent as from 1 August 2001.

Records must be kept for three years and you complete your obligation as your own tax collector when you post the completed form and appropriate payment to the VAT man.

PAYE

Employers are responsible for deducting PAYE from wages and paying it over monthly to the Revenue – including PAYE from their own salary. Small employers with a monthly bill for PAYE and NICs of less than

£1,500 a month can pay quarterly. Deductions are based on the tax code number and the Revenue supply tables. Employees must receive Form P60 with details of pay and tax deductions at the end of the tax year. Form P35 goes to the Revenue, summarising their tax and NICs. Leaving employees must receive a P45 – part of which goes to your tax office – to hand to their new employer to ensure the tax record continues.

National Insurance Contributions (NICs)

All employees and anyone employing them pay NICs. Rates for the tax year 2000/01 are shown in Table 6.7.

Table 6.7 National Insurance Contributions for 2000/01

	Employer	**Employee**
Sole trader/partner		
Class 2	£2.00 per week	No payment required if you expect earnings to be less than £3,955 pa
Class 4 – on profits of £4,535 to £29,900	7% with £1,775.55 maximum	No payment required if state retirement age is reached by 6 April 2000
Company director/employee		
Class 1 (not contracted out)		
Payable on earnings		
Up to £87	Nil	Nil
£87.01–£575	11.9%	10%
Over £575	11.9%	£48.80 maximum
Men 65 and over and women 60 and over	as above	Nil

Exemption applies if state retirement age is reached by 6 April 2001.

- As from 4 June 2001 the rate of employers' NICs is reduced from 12.2 per cent to 11.9 per cent.
- Class 4 NICs will be deferred if you can show you are likely to pay more than a total of £1,746.95 in Class 1 and 2 NICs.
- Class 2 NICs are deferred if you are likely to pay more than £2,432.70 in Class 1 NICs.

Pensions

The sole trader or partner is entitled to the self-employed person's State flat-rate pension at retirement age which is not related to previous income. Premiums on self-employed policies are not allowable against income.

Your company can 'contract out' of the State Pension Scheme. If you do nothing, you have 'contracted in' and 'not contracted out contributions' apply and employees receive the State earnings-related pension.

If you contract out, you pay lower rates on higher incomes and make your own pension arrangements and there is tax relief on premiums which varies with the age of the taxpayer and the pension. For personal pension plans the relief is 17.5 per cent for those aged 35 or under, increasing to a maximum of 40 per cent for those aged 61 and over. There is a limit on the amount of earnings taken into account in calculating the maximum contributions qualifying for relief which for 2001/02 is £95,400 excluding Department of Social Security contributions for employees contracted out of the State Earnings Related Pension Scheme (SERPS).

Personal pension premiums paid on or after 6 April 2001 attract immediate basic rate tax relief at source. Premiums paid on 6 April 2000 can be carried back to 2000/01 to use up unused relief from earlier years.

Statutory references

These have been kept to a minimum; further details are available from the Inland Revenue, HM Customs & Excise, the Benefits Agency and the Department of Social Security

Capital Allowances Acts 1968 and 1990
Companies Act 1985
Finance Acts 1965, 1966, 1972, 1975, 1976, 1980, 1982, 1984 to 2000
Finance Act (No 2) 1997
Income and Corporation Taxes Acts 1970 and 1988
Taxation of Chargeable Gains Act 1992
Social Security Act 1998
Social Security Contributions and Benefits Act 1992 as amended
Value Added Tax Act 1994

7

Insurance

Insurance is a gamble and you can cover almost any risk at a price. The only real difference between insurance and placing a bet is that insurance contracts are enforceable in English law.

The insurance contract

First you submit a proposal – application – to a broker or insurer giving details of the risk. The insurance contract is complete when your offer is unconditionally accepted, although the insurer can accept subject to payment of the premium. Non-marine policies can be agreed verbally if the items, the sum insured and the risks are specified. With other insurance you can, if those terms are agreed, be covered pending formal acceptance but the insurer can withdraw after making enquiries.

Cover can be arranged informally on issue of a cover note. This is a temporary contract, distinct from the formal policy, unless the insurer combines them by sending the cover note on receipt of the premium as a 'deposit receipt'. Temporary cover notes renewing existing policies do not extend cover automatically and may be only an offer to insure, requiring acceptance. The note becomes a deposit receipt when the premium is paid. Some policies are self-extending but if not, a new policy must be agreed, unless cover is renewed on the 'usual' or 'previous' terms.

The law of the contract

If you trade abroad insurance may be governed by foreign law, unless the contract states it is to be governed by English law. Who receives the payment depends on the law of the place where the money is payable – whether money is owed is governed by the law of the contract but who receives it is governed by the law where it is to be paid out. Money is usually payable where insurers carry on business but life policies pay out in accordance with the law where the deceased was domiciled on death.

Terms and conditions

Legally, insurance contracts are contracts of *uberrimae fidei*. That is, they are made in 'the utmost good faith' and the parties must disclose everything affecting the risk. A mistake or inadequate disclosure may amount to misrepresentation and changes to the risk may invalidate the policy.

You can agree values initially under a 'valued policy'. Claims are based on that value but usually cover is limited to a specific amount, which is the maximum you can claim. Overvaluation can lead to cancellation and if no values are agreed you can usually claim the market value or the cost of repair or restoration to the limit of the sum insured, subject to averaging.

Most policies include an *average clause* that restricts claims to current market values, taking account of depreciation, which is usually less than replacement value. You can insure for replacement cost but premiums are higher.

If cover is only for loss of goods or damage to premises, there is no claim for loss of profits, loss of rent or loss of custom unless included in the policy.

Because you acquire new items to replace those depreciated in value by use, a discount on claims for goods lost or destroyed is usually included but you can, if this is possible, require the insurer to pay for repairs instead.

Most policies set out terms and conditions, some describe legal effects and enlarge or restrict rights and obligations. On careful and expert reading you may discover you are entitled to damages if a claim is refused.

Cover

Claims are based on abnormal circumstances. Normal wear and tear and inherent vice – natural behaviour of the item insured – are usually excluded, even under 'all risks' cover (which means loss or damage caused in the circumstances set out in your policy). Most risks can be covered for a price but riot, act of God, civil commotion and war are usually excluded. Accident policies cover accidents caused by carelessness, including the insured's, but deliberate damage is only covered if someone else is responsible.

Only risks occurring during the currency of the policy are covered. Transit risks are usually covered from the beginning to the end of the trip but you should check that loading and unloading, goods in storage, loaded overnight or unattended are covered and all methods of transport are included, in case there is an unforeseen change of route.

The time of loss is the time of the accident, whenever discovered, except in marine insurance, or if arising from an accident outside the period of cover. Causation can therefore be crucial.

Claims are based on one direct, operative cause – the 'proximate' cause – which cannot be an excepted risk or outside the risk period.

Goods in transit

If you use a 'common carrier', that is, public transport, the carrier insures your goods and is liable for their loss or damage, unless due to an act of God or the Queen's enemies or unless there is an agreement to the contrary. There is no contract between you and the carrier, and the amount you can claim is minimal. You can claim the full value if you declare the value on delivery, but the costs of carriage will then be raised accordingly.

Carriage by sea

Contracts for carriage by sea and contracts of affreightment are incorporated into in a bill of lading (see p 67) or a charter party, and you must insure the goods yourself.

If you deal directly with shippers and need to use all the space in a ship, the contract is usually contained in a bill of lading. This is a document signed by the ship owners, or on their behalf, stating that your goods have been shipped on a specified ship or have been received for payment; when signed by or on behalf of the carrier the bill of lading is handed to the skipper. The bill and the goods can be transferred by endorsement and delivery of the bill but it is not a negotiable instrument.

If you hire a ship directly from the ship owner to carry your goods, however, your contract is a contained in a 'charter party' which can be either:

- a voyage charter party – covering carriage in a specified ship from a named port to a named port for one or more voyages;
- a time charter party – covering carriage for a specified period; or
- a charter party by demise – where you have complete control of the ship, its navigation and your own master and crew.

Marine insurance

Marine insurance covers 'maritime perils' incidental to 'marine adventures', ie ships and goods exposed to maritime perils and lost or damaged goods travelling by sea. You can extend the cover to inland waters.

Marine insurance contracts are made when the proposal is accepted by the insurer. Usually a document is issued – the 'slip' – which is a short memorandum of the contract when it is accepted by the underwriter. The broker acts as your agent and offers the slip to insurers, such as the underwriting syndicates at Lloyds. Each agent of the syndicate writes a line, ie accepts a limited amount of risk – *pro tanto* – until the full amount on the slip is covered. The slip itself is an offer and the signature of the underwriters, through their agents, is their *pro tanto* acceptance. There is therefore a separate and binding contract between you and each underwriter even before the full amount on the slip is covered, although you cannot sue on the slip until the policy is issued.

You can take out:

- *voyage policies* – cover from port to port;
- *time policies* – cover for a specified period;

- *mixed policies* – cover for a specified voyage and period;
- *valued policies* – cover for a specified value;
- *unvalued policies* – where the value is calculated according to a formula and subject to the limit of the sum insured;
- *floating policies* – where details are defined by later declaration.

In marine policies, the value of claims is the value when the goods were insured, not their value at the time of loss and, unless expressly excluded, claims are subject to averaging.

Notice of loss

Notice must be given promptly and in accordance with the policy, with sufficient details to enable the insurer to ascertain the nature of the claim. Verbal notice may be accepted but it is advisable to have a written record.

You may have to prove loss, damage and the amount claimed and must usually report loss or theft to the police or appropriate authorities. Insurers often instruct assessors and loss of profits usually requires assessment by auditors.

Settlement

Claims are usually negotiated and, if substantial or complicated, you should instruct assessors. Entitlement under a cover note or after the renewal date depends on the circumstances and the type of insurance. Most insurers will agree to have liability – not the amount of the claim – decided in court even if there is an arbitration clause, unless you expressly agreed to the clause or it is a marine or aircraft policy.

Acceptance must be unconditional but payment can be recovered if the insurer can prove fraud or a mistake of fact.

Usually settlement is in cash and the insurer is entitled to claim lost or damaged goods as salvage.

Insuring business premises

Insuring the premises

A 1774 statute gives insurers the right to insist on rebuilding or reinstating business premises and, unless the policy sets a limit, they cannot limit the cost and work must be completed within a reasonable time. If damage is caused by fire, a landlord or tenant can force the insurer – but not a Lloyd's underwriter – to rebuild or reinstate unless an occupier is responsible. The insurers do not then have to replace trade or tenants' fixtures and can restrict the cost.

Leasehold premises

Landlord or tenant can insure leasehold premises. The tenant's insurable interest is only as tenant in possession, so he can only recover his own loss, unless liable for the value of the entire premises under a repairing covenant or the general law. Rent usually continues to be payable even if the tenant is not required to repair in the event of fire or the premises are destroyed.

The tenant therefore usually insures at the commencement of the lease if he covenants to repair. The tenant is in breach of covenant if renewal premiums are not paid and the landlord can claim damages or, if there is a right of re-entry for breach of covenant, forfeit the lease.

If the tenant is not bound to insure, the landlord must do so but the tenant is liable for increases in the premium due to changes on his own premises and cannot recover under the landlord's insurance although he may be entitled to claim reinstatement under the 1774 Act. If the covenant benefits both landlord and tenant, the landlord must reinstate. You can extend fire cover to include 'special perils', including explosions, earthquakes and overflowing of water tanks, apparatus or pipes, on a replacement or reinstatement basis, as well as architects' and surveyors' fees, the building contents, stock, plant, machinery, fixtures and fittings and the removal of debris. Fire insurance can also be restricted, but you are usually covered for your own damage by explosion on your premises but not necessarily for damage to other buildings unless caused by the fire itself.

Types of insurance

Burglary insurance

This covers theft involving forceful or violent entry and the insurer usually requires the premises to be properly protected.

Engineering insurance

Inspection by 'competent' engineers required by the Factories Act is offered by specialist insurers.

Money insurance

Insurance against loss of cash covers loss by any cause except theft by employees (insurable under a fidelity bond or policy – see below) and can include personal assault.

Insuring goods

Claims on goods, other than depreciation, depend on whether they are at your risk (see pages 94 and 95) and rights may have to be ceded to the insurer. You can insure before you buy under a 'floating policy' covering 'all the goods in the warehouse or otherwise ascertainable' for a fixed amount, a 'declaration policy' for goods to be declared from time to time, or an 'open policy' insuring against all risks by sea and land. There are several commercial variants, including sellers' insurance inclusive CIF (cost, insurance, freight) for the buyer's benefit and FOB (free on board) insurance where the buyer pays premiums. You should check insurance and sales documents to ensure you are adequately covered.

Liability insurance

Liability insurance covers liability to employees and the general public as employer, owner and occupier of a building. Public liability insurance usually covers compensation for injury, disease or damage to the public and can be extended to cover accidents caused by defective goods but not injury to your own employees, damage to your property if you are in occupation and some kinds of liability under commercial contracts.

Because you are usually liable for injuries sustained by employees at work, you must be covered by appropriate insurance with authorised insurers, unless you employ only family or independent contractors. The certificate of insurance must be displayed on the premises and details of injuries kept in an accident book.

Personal accident and/or sickness insurance

Schemes can be set up to provide employees with accident and sickness cover and health insurance.

Motor vehicle insurance

Legally you must carry 'road traffic cover', indemnifying you only against compensation for death or injury to third parties. 'Third-party cover' indemnifies you for damage to third-party property and can be extended to loss and damage to your own vehicle. Comprehensive cover also includes accidental damage to your vehicle.

You must inform the insurer if vehicles are used for business purposes. Even under road traffic cover you are usually insured personally to drive any vehicle but you should check to make sure your policy is automatically transferred if you change your vehicle, it is stolen or destroyed, or if you make a claim.

Fidelity bonds and policies

Employees' theft, breach of confidence and fraud are covered by fidelity bonds and policies. They usually apply to particular employees in a stated capacity for a fixed period and loss arising from default within the period is covered, even if discovered after it. It is not usually necessary to give notice of suspicion.

Credit insurance

Debts are usually insured on the basis of an indemnity (but see pages 111–12 for business done abroad). Cover can be for default on the due date or in specified circumstances. Unless claiming an unpaid balance, you do not usually have to sue the debtor or enforce a security. Your rights are transferred to the insurers on payment but you may have to carry part of the loss. Debts and uncompleted contractual performance can also be covered by guarantees and sureties. Under a guarantee you are guaranteed payment but a surety pays you on default and the principal debt remains unaffected.

Insurance against legal claims

Insurance is available to cover most civil claims brought against you in the courts, including legal costs.

Directors and auditors

Companies can indemnify officers and auditors for liability in some civil or criminal proceedings provided judgment is given in their favour, relief is granted by the court, or they are acquitted. If the Articles permit, additional insurance is obtainable to cover unindemnifiable risk.

Insuring key personnel

You can insure against loss caused by the death of senior management, to provide cash to buy out a deceased partner's share, or to engage someone to take over management.

Disputes

The Insurance Ombudsman deals with insurance disputes and details are available from the Insurance Ombudsman Bureau's office.

Statutory references

Companies Act 1989
Defective Premises Act 1972
Employers' Liability (Compulsory Insurance) Act 1969
Employers' Liability (Defective Equipment) Act 1969
Factories Act 1961
Fire Prevention (Metropolis) Act 1774
Marine Insurance Act 1906
Occupiers' Liability Act 1957 and 1983
Sale of Goods Act 1979

8 *Employers and employees*

When you take on employees the law may take an active part in the business. You may have to comply with industrial practice and collective bargaining agreements. The network of legislation is studded with fines and penalties and contravention can prove far more expensive than taking preventive measures.

Employers' obligations

The employment legislation covers all employees, including part-timers, except for:

- close family;
- non-executive directors;
- trainees under youth training schemes;
- employees working abroad;
- the self-employed.

Directors as 'office-holders' are excluded unless they are clearly employees – for instance, there is a service contract.

Self-employed workers are excluded from employment protection and they also have their own responsibilities under health and safety legislation. It is therefore important to know whether your workers are employed by you or by themselves. Key criteria include the job description, when and how payment is made, who pays tax and National Insurance, how far and to what extent the employee is integrated into your business and whether the 'employer' provides equipment and who takes a profit or loss on the work.

It is the local authority that supervises children's employment. Children of 13 or over must not work during school hours, before 7 am or after 7 pm on school days but they can work part time for two hours on school days and Sundays.

Employee protection

Protection gives rights to guarantee and redundancy payments, minimum periods of notice, compensation for unfair dismissal and other rights listed below. Once agreed, all employees (including part-timers) are entitled to the same sick leave, pensions, holidays, staff discount and share option benefits, including regular part-timers and casual part-time employees working on a day to day basis for over three months.

Within two months of starting work, employees must have a *written statement* giving details of employer and employee, a job description, the place of work, the date of starting work and what other work, if any, forms part of the 'continuous period of employment' (increasing the qualifying period for protection under the legislation). Working hours must be set out, the amount and time of payment, disciplinary procedures (but not grievance procedures if there are less than 20 employees), details of relevant collective agreements, pension rights, holiday and sick pay, length of notice and details of any contracting-out certificate (relating State pensions to earnings); length of employment must be included for temporary employees. Details of pension schemes, sick pay, disciplinary rules and procedures and notice can instead be in another reasonably accessible document. Employees must receive written notification of changes within a month of the change.

Pay statements must give details of gross and net pay, with details of the amounts and reasons for deductions.

After four weeks' work you and your employees are entitled to a week's notice. After two years employees are entitled to a week's notice for each year of continuous work to a maximum of 12 weeks but they can take payment in lieu.

Hours of work

The EU's Working Time Directive, incorporated into our law, requires workers, other than managing and executive staff and family members to have:

- a minimum daily rest period of 11 consecutive hours in a 24-hour period;
- a rest break if working longer than 6 hours;
- a minimum rest period in 7 days of 24 consecutive hours (plus 11 hours daily rest);
- a maximum average of 48 hours work in 7 days including overtime;
- a maximum of 48 hours average working time in 7 days;
- paid annual leave of at least 4 weeks.

And there are specified restrictions on night workers' hours of work.

According to the European Court, all employees, including those on short-term contracts, are entitled to 4 weeks' annual paid holiday in accordance with the directive. Currently, however, our law requires employees to work for at least 13 weeks before they have any right at all to paid leave.

Contracts of employment

The statement is not a contract but is evidence of some terms in a full service contract. This can be oral or written and should include everything in the statement plus a requirement to follow the safety at work scheme, if any, and works' rules put together after consultation with staff or their representatives. (If rules are included, they must be changed by agreement; if not, they can be changed any time.) Changes are accepted if there is no objection within a reasonable time unless the contract permits variation or it can be implied from conduct or a collective agreement. Objection by resignation may be constructive dismissal and also unfair dismissal.

Wages

If payment is not agreed, reasonable remuneration can be claimed for work done.

Workers must be paid not less than the national minimum wage – currently £3.20 per hour for employees aged 18 to 21 and £3.70 (£4.10 from October 2001) for those aged 22 and over. Here, 'workers' are employees working under a contract of employment or agreement whereby they undertake to do or perform personally work or services. Clients, customers, the self-employed and members of your family are not workers.

Your records must show payments as an hourly rate, they must be sufficient to show compliance with legislation and must be produced on request to the employee, the enforcement agency, tribunals and courts. The Inland Revenue deals with complaints and can enter premises, inspect records and issue enforcement notices. 'Penalty notices' may be served if the notice is not complied with – the employer will be fined and the employee may be awarded additional pay.

Deductions from the wages of 'workers' – here anyone working as an employee or self-employed, including apprentices but not those working directly for customers or clients – are unlawful unless:

- required or permitted by the law or the contract;
- the worker has given prior written consent.

And you can lawfully deduct:

- reimbursement for overpaid wages and expenses;
- payments made under statutory disciplinary proceedings;
- statutory payments due to a public authority;
- amounts due to third parties under contract – eg TU dues – and to satisfy court orders;
- wages during a strike.

You can also make deductions for cash shortages and stock deficiencies from retail employees' wages to a total of 10 per cent of the gross wage.

Sick pay

You can agree whatever you like about sick pay but employees off sick for at least four consecutive days – including weekends, holidays and days off – can claim Statutory Sick Pay (SSP). SSP is only payable for qualifying days, ie days on which employees are required to work. Nothing is payable for the first three ('waiting') days. Qualifying days during the previous eight weeks when an employee is off sick for at least four consecutive days count towards waiting days and absences of at least four consecutive days link with other absences during an eight-week period. Sickness can be self-certificated on form SC2 but after seven days medical certificates should be provided.

SSP1 must be sent to employees off sick for four or more days who are *not* entitled, or cease to be entitled, to SSP so they can claim Incapacity Benefit.

The daily rate of pay is based on the weekly rate divided by the number of qualifying days in the week for which you pay SSP. Weeks begin on Sunday and each week commencing Sunday that the employee is sick is a separate pay period. SSP is treated like pay, so you must deduct PAYE, tax and NICs. You can also deduct the lawful deductions set out above. When the employee is paid daily or weekly, SSP will be below the NIC lower-earnings limit, but if you make any other payments in the same period – eg wages or occupational sick pay – tax and NICs must be deducted. SSP is included as part of the total year's pay for directors and employees with annual earnings periods.

Records must be kept on Inland Revenue forms, your own computerised forms or magnetic tape and retained for at least three years. Forms and SSP2 records sheets are obtainable free of charge from the Inland Revenue, but you can use computerised forms if they include the necessary information.

If employees have more than one job, earnings from each job count separately for NICs and you can share SSP payments with the other employer. If the employee's other job is working for him- or herself, you are liable for the full amount of SSP.

If at least seven days' SSP is due to an employee who leaves the job, you must give a leaver's statement on SSP 1(L) but this is only needed by a new employer if the employee is sick for at least four consecutive days during the first eight weeks.

Employees not entitled to SSP include those under 16 and over 65, employees on fixed- term contracts of three months or less and those paid less than £87.00 per week (the level at which NICs currently become payable).

SSP ceases to be payable after 28 weeks or the employee becomes entitled to Maternity Pay or Allowance. You can recover payments under the Percentage Threshold Scheme (PTS) if total SSP payments exceed Class 1 NICs for the tax month less contracted-out rebate, if any, multiplied by 13 per cent of your NIC liability for the tax month. Records of total gross Class 1 NICs and SSP payments in each month should be entered in your Inland Revenue payslip booklet P30BC, form P32 or your pay records. You can deduct the amount you are entitled to recover from your contributions to the Inland Revenue. If you are entitled to recover more than the contributions due, you can deduct the excess from PAYE income tax due that month, entering the excess in the National Insurance box of the payslip, preceded by the letter 'M' (for minus), but *do not* alter the amount entered for PAYE tax.

Even if you have opted out, you can still recover payments up to the amount of SSP due under the PTS and deduct it from payments to the Inland Revenue Accounts Office, but details must be recorded on forms P14 and P35. Write directly to the Inland Revenue Accounts Office at the address on your P30(BC) if you need to recover the payments as a matter of urgency.

Details of the SSP scheme, explanatory booklets and forms are obtainable from the Inland Revenue.

You can opt out of the SSP scheme for all or part of your workforce if your occupational sick pay (OSP) scheme offers equivalent or better benefits whether or not your scheme is formalised. You can pay on an informal or discretionary basis, or you can pay the normal wage. You can also choose to pay OSP for a limited period and then opt an employee back into SSP.

You do not have to inform the Revenue if you opt out and you can still claim the amount you could have recovered under the percentage threshold scheme, provided you keep proper records.

This means that you do not have to keep two sets of records (for OSP and SSP) although in practice you must still keep most of your SSP records.

You can demand full *medical reports*, but employees must be informed that they have a right to approve or amend the report or, having seen it, to refuse to supply it, unless it refers to a third party. The doctor is entitled to refuse to make amendments or to permit disclosure on the ground that it would prejudice the employee's health.

If you suspect malingering, the Inland Revenue will assist, provided the employee has been off sick for four or more short periods in 12 months. A letter to the local Inland Revenue (NICs) office with a report from the employee's doctor may persuade it to ask for a medical examination. The Inland Revenue will send the result of the examination to you stating whether there are reasonable grounds for the absences or whether the employee is incapable of work. If the employee is capable of work, you must decide whether or not to continue paying SSP. The same applies if the employee refused to disclose a doctor's report. If you stop the payments at this stage, the employee is entitled to hear your reasons for doing so. If requested, you must give a written explanation and the employee can seek the Inland Revenue's formal decision as to entitlement to SSP.

Trade union agreements

Employees can belong to any union even if it is not the union with sole representational rights. Payment of subscriptions must be authorised by members at least once every three years and employees can participate in TU activities as agreed with you or as provided in the union membership agreement.

You are entitled to at least seven days' written notice of official industrial action. After having given notice and before taking action, there must be a postal ballot of members. Unions are not responsible for members' unofficial activities but they are liable for interference leading to breach of commercial contracts unless industrial action is in contemplation or furtherance of a trade dispute. They cannot bring in outsiders and picketing is only permitted at or near the employees' place of work. You may be able to bring proceedings if industrial action is unlawful.

Anti-discrimination legislation

You must not discriminate against full- or part-time employees because of colour, race, ethnic or national origin, sex or marital status. Discrimination based on sexual orientation is probably already unlawful. It is specifically prohibited under a European directive to be incorporated into our law by 2 December 2003, which also prohibits discrimination based on religion and belief. The directive making discrimination based on age and disability unlawful must be incorporated into our law by 2 December 2006.

But you can insist on employing men or women for specific jobs if their sex is a genuine occupational qualification, it is justified by the nature or circumstances of the job, or the employee is required to work or live in a private home.

Women and men are entitled to be paid the same if doing the same or equivalent work, although economic factors affecting the business may justify paying different wages when they are not employed contemporaneously. They must also be treated in the same way in relation to employee-related benefit schemes and they have parity in occupational pensions for payments relating to employment after 17 May 1990, unless claims have been made earlier.

Maternity benefits

Pregnant employees can take reasonable paid time off for antenatal care. They are entitled to at least 14 weeks' unpaid statutory maternity leave and if they cannot return to work because of redundancy, they must be offered suitable alternative employment.

Statutory Maternity Pay (SMP)

Employees with two years' continuous employment can claim 18 weeks' Statutory Maternity Pay (SMP) from the employer, even if they do not intend to return to work, provided their average weekly earnings are not less than the lower earnings limit for NICs (currently £87.00). Payments are at a rate of 90 per cent of the employee's average weekly earnings for the first 6 weeks and £60.20 for the remaining 12 weeks. Pay during additional maternity absence from the end of the statutory period to the end of the 28th week after the birth is subject to agreement and return to work can be postponed for another 4 weeks because of illness or another proper reason. It is proposed that the 18-week period during which SMP is currently payable be extended to 26 weeks in 2003. It is also proposed that fathers be entitled to two weeks' paternity leave.

Employees must notify and confirm the pregnancy, and you can claim reimbursement of 92 per cent of SMP from the total amount of employees' and employers' NICs due to the Inland Revenue Accounts Office.

Small Employers' Relief (SER) is available if you pay or are liable to pay total employers' and employees' gross Class 1 NICs that does not exceed £20,000. If you pay contracted-out NICs, you should deduct your contracted-out rebate from your employer's NICs when calculating whether or not you qualify. Class 1A NICs on company cars and Class 1B NICs PAYE Settlement Agreements are not included.

Records must be kept on Inland Revenue forms, magnetic tape or in computerised form and retained for at least three years. Other forms can be obtained from your Social Security office, but problems are referred to the Inland Revenue. Payments must be noted on employees' Deduction Working Sheets (P11) and End of Year Returns (P14) and on your annual statement, declaration and certificate (P35).

Disabled employees

If you have more than 15 employees, you must not discriminate against disabled persons by refusing to offer them work or treating them less favourably than other employees. If they are at a substantial disadvantage at their place of work, they can require 'reasonable adjustments' to be made to the premises.

Unless the work is dangerous, 3 per cent of the workforce must be registered disabled if you have more than 20 employees: premises and working arrangements must be appropriately altered.

Employees with criminal records

Applicants for work need not disclose 'spent' convictions – ie with a sentence of more than two and half years' imprisonment, 'spent' after periods of up to ten years – but you can fairly dismiss for failure to disclose un-spent convictions.

Exposure to health risks

After working for four weeks employees can claim up to 26 weeks' pay if exposed to some health risks, unless they are unable to work or unreasonably refuse alternative work.

Guarantee and redundancy payments

Unless they are seasonal or casual workers, apprentices, over retirement age or have given written notice under a contract of at least two years, there is a trade dispute or they unreasonably refuse alternative work, employees with you for four weeks can claim guarantee payments after 12 weeks without work for every day without work. The maximum claim is £16.70 for a maximum of five days in a three-month period unless there is a collective agreement.

Redundancy payments can be claimed when lay-off or short-time work lasts for more than four weeks or more than six in 13. You can agree to pay or, by counter-notice in response to a request, state you reasonably expect to be able to provide at least 13 weeks' continuous work and if there is then no work the employee is entitled to payments. Employees redundant after two years' continuous work can claim even if they volunteer for redundancy or immediately find other employment. Claims must be made within six months and are as follows:

- half a week's pay for employees between 18 and 22;
- a week's pay for employees over 22;
- one and a half weeks' pay for employees over 41;

for each year of employment. Employees over the age of 65 are not entitled to redundancy payments, and the amount is reduced for each complete month the employee is over 64. Pay includes overtime and there is a maximum amount of 20 years' employment at a maximum of £210 per week for 30 weeks.

If independent trade union members are affected, you must consult their representatives before dismissal, giving reasons and stating how many and which employees are to be made redundant. You must do all you can to comply with the requirements if there is insufficient time for full consultation.

Directors or shareholders can authorise additional payments for employees when a company is taken over or wound up.

Employees' obligations

The law assumes that employer and employees enjoy each other's trust and confidence. Employees must follow lawful and reasonable orders and take proper care of your property and must not disclose your industrial and trade secrets unless required to do so by the law.

These belong to the employer if made in the course of employment. Employees should sign agreements to protect you against disclosure of confidential information and from competition but the courts will not enforce one which effectively stops them making a living and you cannot stop disclosure to the Revenue or FIMBRA. If you repudiate the agreement, you cannot enforce the restrictions put on the employee.

References

You do not have to supply references. An employee can sue on a bad reference, but there is no claim if it is true and made without malice. If the reference is too favourable, you may be liable to a new employer if the employee is unsatisfactory.

Inducing breach of the contract of employment

Persuading someone to leave a job is actionable by the ex-employer as an inducement to breach of contract.

Disciplinary powers of management

Some disciplinary powers are specified under the employment and earlier legislation. Procedures should be fair and worked out with the employees and their representatives. Employees should know who can take action and in what circumstances. They must have an opportunity to defend themselves and a right to appeal to a senior level of management or independent arbitration. Fines can only be imposed for breaches of discipline likely to cause loss and must be fair and reasonable. Deductions from pay can be made in connection with disciplinary proceedings under statute. Procedures should be set out in a rule book and employees should acknowledge agreement by signature. Details should also be included in contracts of employment or notices and, unless based on trade practice, in collective agreements.

Codes of practice

Some disciplinary powers and procedures are set out in codes of practice issued under the employment legislation. These, and codes under the health and safety legislation are available from The Stationery Office. Government codes of practice can be obtained from the Department for Education and Skills. The Equal Opportunities Commission and the Commission for Racial Equality issue codes covering anti-discrimination legislation and TUC codes cover trade disputes and payments to political funds. The codes do not have the force of law but are taken into consideration in the event of disputes.

Dismissal

The unfair dismissal provisions apply to full and part-time employees who have worked for you for two years, except those:

- over normal retiring age – 65 or the agreed age of retirement (which must be the same for all employees);
- working or residing abroad.

There is no two-year qualifying period and dismissal or redundancy is unfair for the following 'inadmissible' reasons:

- pregnancy or childbirth;
- sex or race discrimination;
- for taking appropriate action on health or safety grounds – selection for redundancy on this ground is also unfair dismissal;
- TU membership or TU activities.

But you can fairly dismiss employees on strike on written notice stating if they do not return to work within a specified time they will be dismissed and the dismissal is during the strike.

Retail shop employees must be given a written statement setting out their rights in connection with Sunday work within two months of engagement. They cannot be dismissed or penalised for refusing to work on Sundays if this was agreed at the outset or if they agreed before 26 August 1994 to work Sundays. If Sunday work is agreed, the employee can give later written notice of objection which is usually effective after three months.

Fair dismissal is based on one of the following:

- the employee's capabilities or qualifications (*if* required by the contract);
- misconduct – eg persistent drunkenness or dishonesty;
- redundancy – 'Last in first out' (LIFO) is usually safest and fairest;
- the employee cannot continue work without breaking the law – eg a driver loses his driving licence;
- some other substantial reason – eg going into business in competition with you;
- on transfer of the business: for economic, technical or organisational reasons (see page 155).

Putting an employee in an untenable position, thereby compelling him to resign – eg moving a senior executive into a very small office although paying the same salary – may be unfair and also wrongful dismissal.

You must act fairly and reasonably and the employee must have a chance to defend him or herself. Instant dismissal is rarely justified and warnings, if possible written, should be given, with details of the complaint and stating that dismissal will follow if there is no improvement. Usually you must give a second written warning before you can consider suspension or dismissal. Reasons for dismissal must be sent to the employee within 14 days of dismissal.

If unfair, an industrial tribunal will, if practicable, order reinstatement in the same job, re-engagement in a similar job, or compensation which consists of a basic award of half a week's pay to one-and-a-half weeks' pay at a maximum of £240 per week for each year of employment, depending on age and length of service for a maximum of 30 years, with a minimum of £3,100 and a maximum of £7,200.

The basic award for trade union- and health and safety-related dismissal and for employees excluded or expelled from a trade union is £5,500.

A compensatory award that is just and equitable in the circumstances is a maximum of £51,700, but there is no limit if the employee was unfairly dismissed or made redundant because of health and safety concerns or public interest disclosure ('whistleblowing').

If the tribunal's order for reinstatement or re-engagement is ignored or if dismissal is for sex or racial discrimination, an additional award of between 26 and 52 weeks' pay at a maximum of £240 per week to a maximum of £12,480 is possible.

Part of the compensatory award in unfair dismissal cases compensates an employee for loss of earnings to the date of the tribunal hearing. The employee may, however, have already received unemployment benefit or income support for this period. The tribunal will therefore order the employer to pay a specified amount of the employee's award to the Benefits Agency to avoid 'double payment' to the employee.

The employee must mitigate his or her loss and seek alternative employment and the amount may be reduced if the employee unreasonably refuses reinstatement, has found other work, or conduct was a contributory factor.

If the employee loses, he or she does not have to pay your legal costs unless the tribunal decide the allegations were serious or unfounded, but you may be able to obtain payment of all or some of your costs if the dismissal was because of TU pressure.

The tribunal can also award damages for breach of the employment contract of up to £25,000.

E-mail and your employees

If your employees have agreed that you can monitor their e-mails, you can legally dismiss them for sending and receiving e-mails that do not relate to their work. You need their specific agreement, preferably under a clause in the statement or contract of employment that gives you the right to access and monitor all messages created, sent, received and stored on your systems, or a clause stating that e-mails are not the employees' private property and there should be no expectation of privacy. In addition, you should try to inform everyone who uses your systems that you can monitor and record e-mails.

Bear in mind, however, that the law – under the Regulatory Investigative Powers Act 2000 (RIPA) – only came into force in July 2000. It has yet to be tested in the courts and may be dismissed due to it conflicting with the Data Protection Act 1998 and possibly also with the implied contractual relationship of mutual confidence and trust between employer and employee and the employees' right to privacy under the Human Rights Act 1998.

Your best course therefore is to agree sensible guidelines on good business practice and guidelines to safeguard employees' privacy and your business interests, and include an appropriate consent clause in individual statements and contracts of employment.

Watch the press for reports of the first tribunal decisions under RIPA.

Wrongful dismissal

If you break a term of the individual contract of employment the employee can claim damages for wrongful dismissal in the civil courts under the general law which may amount to far more than compensation for unfair dismissal. Damages here are based on what the employee loses and expects to lose by instant unemployment and he or she must seek comparable alternative employment to minimise loss. If the employee instead chooses to take a claim to the employment tribunal, the maximum amount of an award for breach of contract is £25,000.

But whether the claim is unfair and/or wrongful dismissal, you cannot be forced to take an employee back and you always have the choice of paying compensation instead.

Offences and penalties

It is a criminal offence to refuse to pay the minimum wage, fail to keep proper records or to obstruct officers making enquiries under the legislation. There are fines of up to £1,000 for failing to pay and keep records of SMP and SSP, and for failing to provide information related to claims for

SMP, SSP, Incapacity Benefit, Maternity Allowance or Severe Disablement Allowance, plus a daily fine of £40 until you have put things right. A maximum of £5,000 or three months' imprisonment is the additional penalty for knowingly providing, or allowing to be provided, false documents or information relating to claims and compensation. Fines are also imposed for non-compliance with the anti-discrimination legislation.

Statutory references

Access to Medical Reports Act 1988
Companies Act 1985
Contracts of Employment Act 1972
Copyright, Designs and Patents Act 1988
Disability Discrimination Act 1995
Disabled Persons (Employment) Act 1944
Employment Acts 1980, 1982, 1989 and 1990
Employment of Children Act 1973
Employment Protection Act 1975
Employment Protection (Consolidation) Act 1978
Employment Rights Act 1999
Employment Rights Act 1996
Employment Subsidies Act 1978
Equal Pay Act 1970
Factories Act 1961
Health and Safety at Work Act 1974
Human Rights Act 1998
Industrial Tribunals Act 1996
Race Relations Act 1976
Regulatory Investigative Powers Act 2000
Rehabilitation of Offenders Act 1974
Sex Discrimination Acts 1975 and 1986
Social Security Acts 1975 and 1989
Social Security Contributions and Benefits Act 1992
Sunday Trading Act 1994
Trade Union and Labour Relations (Consolidation) Act 1992
Trade Union Reform and Employment Rights Act 1993
Wages Act 1986

9

Trading

This chapter covers the law of sale of goods and consumer credit, which affect the day-to- day search for profits. Like the law of landlord and tenant and insurance, they are based on contract law.

Contracts

Contracts are agreements between willing parties who exchange promises, eg a promise to deliver goods in return for a promise to pay. The promises *plus* implied terms make up the contract and contract law dictates the remedies for non-performance.

Theoretically, and with important exceptions, oral contracts are as good as written ones but it is better and safer to incorporate business arrangements into written contracts.

Some agreements, including some leases and business contracts, must be written and state that the document is intended to be a deed and both parties must sign (execute) it. One witness is sufficient unless signing on behalf of someone else (eg a company), when there must be two. Sealing, ie sticking a red seal at the foot of the document, is only necessary when required by a company's Articles but the deed must be delivered (handed over).

Only the parties are liable under the contract but agents can pass liability to a principal (as directors do with the company).

Third parties, however, can now claim the same rights and remedies as the contracting parties if the contract specifically gives them rights or if it was made for their benefit. The third party must be identifiable by name or description, and may have to share rights and remedies with a contracting party. If they have rights, they cannot be deprived of them without their consent unless the contract provides for it. There are, however, no third party rights in employment contracts, contracts for the carriage of goods and contracts relating to negotiable instruments (that is, cheques, bills of exchange, etc – see pages 107–09).

Contracts for business abroad made via e-mail may be governed by foreign law. They should therefore state they are governed by English law for convenience, speed and to save costs. Otherwise where the case is heard may have to be decided in accordance with the Rome Convention. And you may have to pursue judgment through foreign courts anyway, if there is no property here to satisfy the claim.

Arbitration

You can agree to have disputes settled by arbitration which is becoming increasingly popular. There may be considerable savings in costs, particularly in landlord and tenant and commercial disputes. Information is available from the Centre for Dispute Resolution (CEDR) (see page 159 for contact details).

Buying and selling for cash

If goods are sold for cash the transaction is governed by the sale of goods legislation and the custom of the trade.

Business buyers have partial protection. They can safely assume the seller owns the goods and the parties cannot be totally unreasonable – a seller with a monopoly will probably be unable to exclude the statutory quality guarantee.

Consumers have full protection: goods must be of satisfactory quality, fit for the purposes for which goods of that kind are commonly supplied, taking into account the price and other relevant circumstances. 'Quality' includes:

- the state and condition of the goods;
- appearance and finish;
- safety and durability;

and they must be free from minor defects except for defects:

- drawn to the buyer's attention;
- discoverable on inspection, if the buyer was given a chance to inspect them;
- apparent on reasonable inspection of a sample in sale by sample.

And they must correspond with samples, descriptions and display items. The protection covers some agreements to hire goods and contracts for services, including repairs and maintenance where work must be done in a reasonable time, with reasonable care and skill and, if no price is agreed, at a reasonable price.

New regulations now further protect the consumer. Consumer contracts must be in 'plain intelligible language' and 'unfair' terms are unlawful and void, which here means contrary to good faith and significantly weighting the contract against the consumer. The consumer can now, for instance, sue directly on a penalty clause even if the contract states that he has no right to do so.

Selling to consumers can bring liability for others' mistakes, eg for inadequate manufacturer's instructions.

Liability for quality and quantity can be restricted or excluded but the law more readily permits a limitation of liability. Only specific wording excludes liability for negligence or non-performance and in dealing with consumers the clause or notice on your premises has no legal effect. Widely framed indemnity clauses are illegal and you are liable for accidents resulting in personal injury or death. But liability for financial loss and damage can be restricted if the contractual clause or notice is reasonable in the circumstances. Here the bargaining strength of the parties and the price are relevant in business transactions and consumers have more protection.

Importer, manufacturer, packager, carrier, installer, distributor, retailer, hirer and anyone putting names or labels on goods is strictly (automatically) liable to consumers for death, personal injury and loss or damage to property exceeding £275. Defences include compliance with the law or scientific and technical knowledge, and liability can be passed up and down the chain of supply. Personal injury claims must be made within three years of the date the claimant knew his rights; a six-year time limit applies to contractual claims. No claim can be made after products have been circulated for ten years.

A manufacturer's guarantee cannot limit liability for negligence or exclude or restrict the consumer's contractual rights.

In commercial transactions you can agree almost anything you like but there are legal limits, eg contravention of EU law renders that part of the agreement void. Unfair or anti-competitive trading – eg price-fixing, exclusive dealing or imposing artificially high prices – infringes our own and/or EU monopolies legislation. In consumer transactions it is an offence to mislead as to price, to pose as a private seller and to infringe safety regulations. But there are exclusions, including food, food stuff, fertiliser, gas supplies, aircraft (except for hang-gliders), motor vehicles, controlled drugs, medicines and tobacco. Defences include a reasonable belief they would not be used in the UK or, for retailers, the goods were not new or you did not believe they were sub-standard.

In deciding if a term is unfair to consumers, all the relevant circumstances at the time the contract was concluded are taken into account, including the nature of the goods and services. An exhaustive and exhausting list of terms considered unfair unless individually negotiated between trader and consumer is set out in the Unfair Terms in Consumer Contracts Regulations 1999. They include terms excluding or limiting liability and allowing the seller or supplier to unilaterally change the terms of the contract or the duration of a fixed-term contract.

Agreeing the contract

First comes the offer. When a firm offer is accepted, the contract is complete. Accepting a specific quantity of specific goods delivered over a fixed period at a fixed price is acceptance of the whole consignment, even if delivered by instalments. A buyer can revoke a contract for a maximum quantity as and when demanded. It is basically a standing offer, each order being placed under a separate contract but goods already ordered must be accepted.

Acceptance by post is received when posted even if not received. Oral, faxed and (presumably, there are no cases on it) e-mailed acceptance is received when heard or seen. Offers to sell can be cancelled any time before being accepted but should be confirmed before selling elsewhere. Acceptance varying an offer – eg by asking for a different quantity – may be a counter-offer, requiring the other side's acceptance. If you do not ask for formal acceptance, goods are accepted unless rejected within a reasonable time or they form part of a 'commercial unit' (see below) but not if a buyer asks for or has agreed to repair or has re-sold them.

Standard terms of business in consumer transactions must be intelligible and consumers can refer to the courts to assess fairness. Business customers are less protected and if both parties use standard terms – eg in order forms and delivery notes – each set may be a counter-offer. The contract may then incorporate the terms of the last document exchanged but unusual or onerous terms are only incorporated if specifically pointed out.

Payment and delivery

The law will not put a whole contract together. Terms of the trade or terms included in previous dealings may be incorporated but if price, quality, size, style and design or content are not agreed, there may be no contract unless omissions are minor details. If price is not agreed, the buyer must pay a 'reasonable' price within a reasonable time. Deposits are usually lost if the buyer does not complete the transaction but part payments must be returned.

The right to claim (statutory) interest at 8 per cent above current bank base rate on debts for goods and services supplied to other traders is now automatically incorporated into business contracts. Interest becomes due the day after the specified date for payment, or the 30th day after delivery, or the 30th day after the purchaser is notified of the debt – whichever is the later.

A contractual term excluding statutory interest is void unless you have agreed a term allowing interest on late payments at a reasonable and substantial rate.

Unless otherwise agreed, you can take delivery when you pay. If nothing is agreed, the law spells out the details as follows.

- You can refuse delivery of more or less than ordered, unless the amount is negligible. If accepted you must pay, *pro rata*, at the contract price.
- If goods are mixed with goods not ordered, you can accept all the goods or only those ordered.
- You can reject all or part of a consignment, including goods under an instalment contract, which does not conform with the contract, *unless* part of a 'commercial unit' and division would impair the goods' value or character – eg parts of a machine – but you may be able to exclude this provision in business transactions.

And you do not have to return rejected goods, although you must notify the seller of rejection.

Payment, unless otherwise agreed, is not due until delivery but if goods are lost or destroyed while at your risk, you may have to pay for them. When you pay, the seller must deliver or pay damages. If unique goods – eg antiques – are involved, the court will order delivery whatever the cost.

If the price is not paid or offered, the seller can retain goods, stop them in transit or sell them elsewhere. After delivery to a carrier, delivery can only be held up if the right has been expressly reserved, unless the carrier is an independent middleman. Delivery of instalment contracts cannot be held up to extract payment for earlier deliveries.

The owner takes the risk and a buyer may own goods before receiving and paying for them. A clause providing goods remain the seller's until paid for – a 'retention of title clause' – protects a seller if a buyer becomes insolvent. This is relatively straightforward for intact goods but provisions covering sale proceeds or materials to be mixed or processed with other goods should be professionally drafted. You may also have to register a charge on the buyer's assets in the Register of Bills of Sale or with the Companies Registry to preserve priority in insolvency.

Ownership passes from seller to buyer as stated expressly or by inference from the contract or surrounding circumstances. If the question is still open ownership depends on whether goods are:

- 'specific' – identified and agreed at the time of the contract;
- 'unascertained' – bought from bulk or of a particular type – eg 12 clocks from stock or 12 clocks.

Goods can also be 'ascertained' by 'exhaustion', for example your purchase of 600 crates of beer sent to you by lorry carrying a consignment of 1,000 crates is yours as soon as the carrier off-loads 400 crates.

Similarly, if you order a quarter of a bulk consignment, eg 8,000 litres of oil, brought to you by tanker, provided the contract of sale identifies your order, you own 2,000 litres of the oil as soon as you have paid for it.

The law then makes the following rules regarding ownership for specific goods:

- if finished and in a deliverable state – the buyer's when the offer is accepted;
- if put into a deliverable state – eg by weighing – the buyer's when notified they are ready to deliver;
- if in the process of construction/manufacture – the buyer's when materials are set aside and identified;
- if held on sale or return – when agreed or accepted, otherwise the buyer's within a reasonable time.

Future or unascertained goods in a deliverable state sold by description are the buyer's when handed to him or a carrier or put in storage.

These rules are contractual only and do not apply to negligence claims.

Misrepresentation

When you are deliberately misled you may be able to claim damages plus reimbursement from the seller, but you must prove the misrepresentation persuaded you to close the deal. You can usually cancel if the seller is careless or genuinely mistaken unless you have agreed to accept the goods or a third party is involved but a specifically worded clause can restrict or exclude liability.

Criminal offences

It is an offence to apply false trade descriptions (FTDs) to goods, or to supply, or offer to supply, goods to which one has been applied. This covers almost any oral or written statement as to quantity, size, manufacture, production, composition, fitness for the purpose, strength, performance and other physical characteristics, testing and approval; previous ownership and other history and dishonesty does not have to be proved. Liability can be disclaimed by an effective disclaimer specifically brought to the buyer's attention.

The provisions also cover a private seller's oral statements and descriptions of services and accommodation, unfair pricing and misleading indications of British origin. You can be vicariously liable for an employee's FTD if you knew it was false when made or read.

Local weights and measures authorities can make test purchases, enter premises and seize goods but usually issue proceedings only if there is a public need for protection. If you are trading for profit you can bring civil proceedings for injunctions to restrain a competitor's further wrongful acts, and you can claim damages and costs.

It is an offence to make, or not correct, uninformative or misleading bargain offers for foods, services, accommodation and facilities (other than investment business).

Misleading advertising

The Director of Fair Trading takes action to stop publication of misleading advertisements for goods and services. The IBA and cable authorities cover commercial TV, radio and cable TV, and traders can be ordered to withdraw advertisements making false claims about food.

Buying and selling on credit

The 1974 Consumer Credit Act and associated legislation apply to credit arrangements for sums between £50 and £15,000, excluding interest but including optional charges and insurance – other than life insurance premiums for loans secured on land. There is no limit if private borrowers are overcharged for credit. Unless agreed otherwise, the agreement between lender and dealer is covered by the sale of goods legislation. The 1974 Act does not apply to company borrowings or to credit arrangements with banks, exempt lenders and companies with a capital of over £250 million with a specialised banking service. Except for EU central banks and exempt lenders, banks must be licensed and comply with banking legislation. No statutory credit can be charged in connection with a credit or security agreement.

Anyone advising on credit terms must have a licence. Licences are available from the Office of Fair Trading and valid for five years at a cost of £70 for sole traders and £175 for partnerships and companies. The Office must be notified of changes affecting the licence – eg new business premises or a change of partners or directors. It is an offence to trade without a licence and unlicensed advisers cannot enforce the agreement, although the borrower can do so. It is also an offence to send out unsolicited credit cards or circulars about credit to anyone under 18. Unsolicited cash loans can only be offered at the lender's business premises.

Borrowers are entitled to have details of their credit references.

With hire purchase, you hire goods with an option to purchase. They remain the seller's until the option is exercised. Conditional sale and credit sale agreements are contracts for the sale of goods at a price paid in instalments. In conditional sales, the borrower owns the goods when all payments are made. In credit sales, he owns them as soon as the contract is made.

Hire purchase and conditional sales are covered by the 1974 Act. Sale of goods legislation applies to credit sales but the rules on acceptance and delivery are the same whether goods are sold on cash or credit.

Most sales on credit are three-cornered: the dealer sells for cash to the lender and the lender sells or hires to the borrower.

The borrower's signed application form is his offer to the lender to buy on credit. When the dealer completes it, the form becomes the dealer's offer to sell to the lender. The lender accepts or rejects both offers and is responsible for the quality guarantee because he sells directly to the borrower.

'Regulated' agreements under the 1974 Act must be signed by the borrower and by or on behalf of the lender and must contain details of:

- the transaction;
- the cost of the credit;
- the right to pay the debt before the agreed date;

- the right, if any, to cancel and to whom notice of cancellation is given – usually within five to 14 days of signing, depending on the type of agreement. This gives the borrower time to consider the transaction.

Cancellation also cancels linked agreements. Items traded in part exchange or their value are returnable within ten days and if the borrower returns goods, he can claim repayment, plus fees or commissions over £1.

The borrower must be given copies of the agreement. If inaccurate the agreement and linked security agreements are enforceable only by court order. In some cases the lender may not be able to enforce it at all.

Special formalities apply to mortgages. The borrower has 14 days to consider the loan which is only enforceable by court order.

If the lender has a right to cancel, notice of cancellation must usually be served on the borrower. The notice must:

- identify the borrower's breach of the agreement, – eg failure to insure goods, so it can be put right;
- state that if it cannot be put right, he can pay specified compensation instead;
- set out the consequences of failing to comply with the notice.

And no further action can be taken by the lender for at least seven days.

No notice is required when the borrower is in arrears or exceeds a credit limit if the lender;

- sues for arrears; or
- restricts the borrower's right to draw on credit.

When over a third of the price is paid, the lender can in some cases only enforce the agreement by court order but the borrower can apply to the court for extra time to pay at any time.

Security for the loan should be included in the agreement or in a document to which it refers. If the borrower provides security, there must be a separate agreement in a prescribed form signed by or on behalf of the guarantor or indemnifier, otherwise it is unenforceable without a court order. If security is given by a third party, eg a recourse agreement between lender and a dealer, it does not have to comply with the Act. Special formalities apply to some security agreements, eg mortgages of goods and assignments of life assurance policies, which are usually only enforceable if the agreement is enforceable, unless an indemnity is for a borrower under the age of 18.

Security and linked agreements are cancelled with the regulated agreement.

Credit buyer's protection

Buyer protection is the same whether you buy for cash or credit but the quality guarantee is backed by the lender. Both dealer and manufacturer are responsible if goods are not checked before delivery.

Consumer hire agreements

These are covered by the Act if within the £15,000 limit and the credit is for more than three months. If annual payments exceed £300, or the goods are specialised goods for the borrower's business, or they have been leased to someone else, the lender can repossess them without a court order but only if he has obtained consent to entry of the premises.

Hiring industrial plant and machinery

Some manufacturers offer their own financing if agreements are outside the £15,000 limit and machinery is often leased. It then remains the manufacturer's or dealer's property and the borrower's cost of hiring is deductible for tax purposes. In credit sales, the borrower owns the goods and can take advantage of capital allowances.

Mortgages

Mortgages are outside the Act and some other loans are specifically exempted but second mortgages on land obtained by private individuals are covered by the Act, whatever the amount.

Doorstep selling

Consumers can refuse to pay for unsolicited goods or services delivered to their home address after an unsolicited visit or telephone call. There is a right to cancel within seven days of contracting and to return unsatisfactory goods within seven days of receipt. The trader must serve notice of the right to cancel within seven days of contracting, stating who must be notified, otherwise the agreement is unenforceable although the consumer's rights are unaffected. Notice of cancellation must be in writing and given personally or by post. Consumers need not return goods until repaid unless a written request is received within 21 days but must take reasonable care of them in the interim. Perishable or consumable goods, goods incorporated into the consumer's property, eg double glazing, or supplied for an emergency need not be returned but the cash price must be paid.

The provisions also cover goods and services other than those discussed at the trader's premises if not usually supplied by him and contracts made while on trips organised by the trader away from business premises. Contracts for work and materials for house repair are covered unless linked to a mortgage but the following are excluded:

- contracts for time share, sale of land and house extensions;
- food, drink, household consumables;
- purchases from trade catalogues if there have been continuous dealings between customer and sales representative;
- some contracts of insurance;
- investment agreements;
- contracts for bank deposits.

Hire purchase, conditional sale agreements and credit exceeding £35 is excluded. The 1974 Act covers credit of between £50 and £15,000 but there is no protection for credit between £35 and £50.

Mail order

Mail order contracts often have a cancellation clause and buyer protection is the same as in cash sales. Unless goods are retained to compel repayment, they must be handed over on written request but the customer does not have to arrange for their return.

Remedies for non-performance

If goods are unsatisfactory:

- Consumers under conditional sales agreements can reject them, even after delivery, unless the transaction has been confirmed.
- If covered by the 1974 Act you can cancel – if the cash price is between £100 and £30,000 supplier and lender are jointly liable to repay deposits.
- In retail sales for cash the customer can refuse credit notes and claim repayment.

A negligent carrier is liable to the owner of damaged goods, even if the owner is not consignor or consignee.

Take advice before claiming for non-delivery. Depending on whether goods have 'perished' (deteriorated), been destroyed or have disappeared, the buyer may be able to claim damages or repayment but may have to pay the seller's necessary expenses. If risk has passed to the buyer, the buyer must pay and claim separately for damages.

If goods do not belong to the seller, you may have to hand them to the owner and claim damages. Goods bought through agents can usually be retained but you should take legal advice before asserting your rights.

If a transaction becomes illegal or there was duress or misrepresentation, there may be a right to rescind (cancel) the contract.

In some circumstances a buyer can claim for consequential loss but reasonable steps must be taken to minimise the loss.

Statutory references

Administration of Justice Act 1985
Arbitration Acts 1950, 1975 and 1979
Banking Act 1979

Bills of Exchange Act 1882
Bills of Sales Acts 1878 to 1882
Companies Act 1985
Competition Act 1980 & 1988
Consumer Arbitration Agreements Act 1988
Consumer Credit Act 1974
Consumer Protection Act 1987
Consumer Safety Act 1978
Contracts (Applicable Law) Act 1990
Contracts (Rights of Third Parties) Act 1999
Deregulation and Contracting Out Act 1994
Fair Trading Act 1973
Late Payment of Commercial Debts (Interest) Act 1998
Latent Damage Act 1986
Law of Property Act 1925
Law of Property (Miscellaneous Provisions) Act 1989
Law Reform (Frustrated Contracts) Act 1943
Limitation Act 1980
Misrepresentation Act 1967
Sale of Goods Act 1979
Sale of Goods (Amendment) Act 1995
Sale of Goods (Implied Terms) Act 1973
Sale and Supply of Goods Act 1994
Supply of Goods and Services Act 1982
Sunday Trading Act 1994
Supply of Goods (Amendment) Act 1994
Supreme Court Act 1981
Trade Descriptions Acts 1968 and 1972
Unfair Contract Terms Act 1977
Unfair Terms in Consumer Contracts Regulations 1999
Unsolicited Goods and Services Act 1974

10 *Cash and credit*

Most trading is for cash or credit and your books are debited and credited with money amounts even if you only deal in paper, with rights and a value varying with the content and creditworthiness of the signatories.

You and your bank

Your creditworthiness essentially depends on your bank which must:

- take reasonable care in conducting your business – they are liable for payments on cheques if they are careless or suspect fraud;
- follow your instructions – they are not obliged to warn of any risks inherent in doing so;
- honour cheques to the limit of the account or overdraft – if they refuse, you may be able to claim damages;
- pay you in cash on request;
- not divulge information about you unless compelled by law or the public interest. If a court requires information, they do not have to inform you.

If asked for advice, their duty of care is very limited and can be further limited by disclaimers of liability.

And you must:

- draw cheques with reasonable care;
- notify the bank of forgeries.

Opening a bank account

When you open the account, the bank requires references. For partnerships, it requires details of the partners and their authority and involvement in the business and a copy of the partnership agreement. Usually, all the partners sign the mandate (agreement) which sets out assets and liabilities and gives instructions as to the conduct of the account – eg who signs cheques and requests advances – and they must confirm that securities to be held by the bank apply to existing and future liabilities and undertake to notify changes in the partners or the agreement. A sole trader's mandate stands until the account is closed or the business wound up. With partnerships it continues even if the partners or the partnership name changes but incoming partners should confirm its terms and outgoing partners remain liable. Cheques drawn by deceased or bankrupt partners must be approved by the partnership, unless the mandate specifies otherwise.

A company account is more complicated because of the protection of limited liability. The bank must see the Certificate of Incorporation, the Memorandum and Articles of Association and a certified copy of the resolution appointing them. The resolution is the company's mandate with the bank and gives instructions about operating the account. Usually the bank supplies a draft resolution to be completed and passed at the first board meeting after arrangements are provisionally agreed. The bank may want a separate resolution covering overdraft facilities, incorporating directors' undertakings given on behalf of the company. The mandate is terminated by board resolution and ends if the account is closed, a receiver appointed, or the company goes into liquidation.

Guarantees

A sole trader's or partner's guarantee, but not the directors', is covered by the Consumer Credit Act if within the £15,000 limit. The guarantees can be open or limited to a fixed amount and become operative when signed by the guarantors. If co-guarantors are insolvent, you can be liable for the whole amount.

Bank guarantees commit you to repay any money owed on all your bank accounts for an indefinite period. The guarantee continues until renegotiated but a deceased guarantor's estate may not be liable so co-guarantors should sign on behalf of 'their heirs, executors and administrators'.

Under other guarantees you can turn to the principal debtor and set off anything already paid and you are then entitled to any security given for the debt. Alternatively you or the creditor can sue the debtor or 'prove' – establish your claim – in his bankruptcy or liquidation.

The sole trader and partner are liable for all business debts but when company debts are paid, directors are only liable if there are problems with floating charges, or fraudulent preferences, or there has been fraudulent or wrongful trading.

Payments

Your cash and paper are negotiable, ie they give rights and obligations which are transferable. If you hold a negotiable instrument you can sue on it. When you give value in good faith – becoming a 'holder in due course' – it becomes valid even if invalid initially, *provided* it is current, unconditional and appears to be properly completed, unless there is a forgery. Trading via bills of exchange and commercial credits is usually confined to larger businesses, although bills are fairly common in some manufacturing trades and heavy industry. Export business is usually done under letters of credit. Historically and currently a bill of exchange permits a seller to be paid when goods are shipped although the buyer does not pay until they are received or sold elsewhere. The period (tenor) of the bill is usually at least three months, a bank or finance house standing as intermediary for payment, and charging a commission for the advance during the period of transit by discounting the payment. Bills can also be accepted, ie by the acceptor's confirmation that the drawee will pay on the due date. The drawer pays the acceptor an agreed percentage of face value, acceptance is endorsed on the bill, the bill becomes freely negotiable and the acceptor becomes primarily liable to the holder.

The main types of negotiable instruments are:

- bills of exchange – a cheque is a bill;
- promissory notes – which include bank notes;
- bankers' drafts – which can be treated as bills or promissory notes.

Bills of lading – receipts for goods sent by sea – are semi-negotiable; once invalid, they remain invalid. Postal and money orders are not negotiable. Money orders are void 12 months after issue.

Negotiable instruments are promises to pay on a specified date. Banks must stop payment on request but you can be sued on the dishonoured promise to pay and your bank is liable if your cheque is wrongly dishonoured. A formal notice of dishonour is usually sufficient to enforce payment through the court at minimal cost. Defences are very limited and if there is a dispute, the debtor must usually pay up and sue in separate proceedings.

Cheques

A cheque is an unconditional order from you (the drawer) to another (your bank, the drawee) to pay a sum of money on demand to a specified person or 'to bearer'.

- If 'to cash or order' it is valid but *not* a cheque because there is no payee.
- Post-dated cheques are valid but banks usually refuse to pay before the due date.
- It is not a continuing security but you remain liable for up to six years (although banks usually return cheques for re-issue after six months).

A cheque crossed 'a/c (or account) payee' with or without 'only' is non-transferable – the crossing can be deleted if you want to transfer it. If you add 'not negotiable' it cannot be negotiated. It can be transferred by endorsement but the endorser cannot pass better title than he has himself – a stolen cheque is valueless – and the bank must give notice of dishonour to endorsers.

Unless post-dated, a cheque comes to life when handed over or the payee is told it is held on his behalf. The holder is the person to whom it is payable (the payee) or the named endorsee or anyone holding a cheque payable 'to bearer'. The holder can alter the crossing but other alterations without the drawer's consent usually invalidate the cheque. If endorsed after alteration, it is valid for the altered amount against the endorser.

Holders take cheques on the same terms as the payee. But if a cheque is not overdue, the holder gives value in good faith, the cheque is regular on its face and the previous holder was entitled to it, the holder becomes a 'holder in due course'. As a 'holder in due course', he is in a stronger position: the cheque can be freely negotiated, payment can be claimed through a non-existent payee and may be claimable on an undated or stopped cheque, or one which the drawer was fraudulently induced to issue.

A bearer cheque is negotiated by handing over – if payable to order it must be endorsed by signing it, the signatory thereby becoming liable for the amount – *and* delivering it to another holder. If no endorsee is named, any name can be written above an endorsing signature. If you are signing or endorsing on behalf of someone else, limit or negative personal liability by signing 'for and on behalf of' your principal or the business *and* describing the capacity in which you sign. Company names must be on all negotiable instruments, endorsements and orders for money and directors endorsing as guarantors are liable to both drawer and holder. One signatory can stop payment on joint company or partnership accounts but one partner's signature is normally sufficient on cheques paid by, or to, the business. Cheques made out to more than one payee must be endorsed by them all, unless one has authority to sign for the others. You can direct endorsees to be paid jointly on the cheque but the face value cannot thereafter be split.

Lending money on an accommodation cheque – by post-dating it and making it payable to someone who makes a loan to a third party – makes you liable to a holder for value.

Banker's drafts

A draft is an order for payment made by the payer's bank and the bank is the drawer and drawee. The amount, place of payment and the name of the beneficiary/payee appear on the draft which when crossed works like a cheque.

Promissory notes

Promissory notes are conditional or unconditional promises to pay on demand, or on a fixed or determinable future date, a fixed sum to, or to the order of, a specified person or to bearer. They can be made payable with interest or in instalments and can provide that if an instalment is unpaid, the full amount becomes due.

A note need only be presented for payment if a place is specified and endorsers are only liable if it has been presented. With some exceptions a note-holder's legal rights and remedies are the same as those of a holder of a bill of exchange.

Bills of exchange

A bill is an unconditional order in writing addressed by one person (the drawer) to another (the drawee), signed by the drawer, requiring the drawee (who, when he signs, becomes the acceptor) to pay on demand or at a fixed or determinable future date, a fixed sum to, or to the order of, a specified person or bearer (the payee). Bills are more easily negotiated than cheques and notes; the right to future payment can be more flexible and is more saleable for immediate cash.

The differences between bills and cheques are as follows.

- Bills can be drawn on anyone, a cheque only on a bank.
- Bills can be payable on demand or in the future – cheques only on demand.
- Bills must be presented for payment, or the drawer and endorser are discharged; a cheque drawer is liable for six years.
- Cheques can be crossed, bills cannot.
- Paying and collecting banks are more exposed when dealing with bills than cheques.
- Unless payable on demand, bills are usually 'accepted'. A cheque is not usually accepted, so the drawer is primarily liable.
- A bill, but only rarely a cheque, can be 'backed' – ie endorsed by someone who is neither drawer nor acceptor and who is liable to a holder in due course. It is backed when sold at a discount for immediate payment, the extra credit cover increasing the discount value.

A bill can be an order to pay from a fund or account, or set out the transaction giving rise to the debt. The value given for payment does not appear on the bill and where it is drawn or payable need not be stated.

A bill can be payable on demand, at sight, on presentation, at a determinable future date, after a fixed period after date or sight, after a fixed period after a specified event *but not on a contingency*. If no time is specified, it is payable on demand.

Interest or payment by instalments can be included with a provision that if an instalment is unpaid the full amount becomes due. If payable in foreign currency the rate of exchange can be specified, otherwise it is calculated according to the rate for sight drafts at the place of payment on the due date.

Bills drawn and payable within the UK or drawn or accepted on a UK resident are inland bills; other bills are foreign. The main difference is that foreign bills must be 'protested' if dishonoured, otherwise protesting may be optional. And inland bills are usually 'sola' ie drawn up in one part. Foreign bills can be drawn in sets of two or three parts (copies), each referring to the others, to protect against loss. You should accept and endorse only one.

Bills must be presented for acceptance and payment on the due date. Strictly, this is only necessary if payable after sight (when acceptance fixes maturity date), if specifically required, or if payable anywhere except the drawee's business or residential address. But they should be presented to secure the drawee's liability and the bills can then be negotiated and discounted – if the drawee refuses acceptance, the holder can immediately turn to the drawer. If the drawee later accepts it, acceptance is backdated to the date on which the bill was first presented for payment.

Bills can be accepted before the drawer signs or when overdue after dishonour except for bills payable after sight which are dishonoured if not accepted. Acceptance can be:

- general – unconditional affirming the drawer's order; or
- qualified – conditional and can be of a partial amount only. The holder can refuse this – unless it is partial acceptance of face value – and treat the bill as dishonoured. Drawer and endorsers are then discharged from liability. Partial acceptance can only be protested as to the balance.

Bills must be presented for payment and acceptance before overdue unless payable on demand, when they can be presented for payment any time. Presentment is usually at the acceptor's or drawer's address and, if agreed, can be by post. All joint acceptors or drawers must be presented with it, unless one has authority to accept for them all. If an acceptor or drawer is bankrupt or dead, the bill can be treated as dishonoured or can be accepted by the trustee in bankruptcy or personal representatives but must first be presented. Although drawer and endorsers are usually discharged from liability if a bill is not presented for payment on the due date, the acceptor remains liable unless he has stipulated it must be presented for payment. If not accepted within a reasonable time, notice of dishonour can be given to drawer and endorsers but if the bill is not 'noted' or 'protested' the right of recourse against them may be lost.

Drawer and endorsers are liable when bills are dishonoured on present-ment for payment. Non-payment of accepted bills gives a right of immediate action against the drawer as acceptor without having to protest the bill or give notice of dishonour.

Generally, notice of dishonour must be given to all parties, in writing or in person, on the day of dishonour or the next working day. Foreign bills require proof of presentation and dishonour. The bill must be re-presented by a notary public and refusal of acceptance or payment is 'noted' on the bill – a declaration (the 'protest') is then made in a separate document. Although not required for inland bills it is safest to do both.

Overseas payments

Overseas business is usually done under letters of credit or documentary or acceptance credits issued by banks or accepting houses, who lend their name where a buyer or seller is unknown or there is doubt about the economic and/or political situation. Interest rates vary with the risk and the trader's credit-standing.

For importers some banks require partial cash cover. The bank issues a letter of credit in favour of the supplier, undertaking to accept his bill drawn on them if accompanied by shipping documents. The supplier's bank buys the bill for cash and sends it with the shipping documents for presentation and acceptance to the importer's bank who releases the documents to the importer, so that he can take delivery.

Overseas customers can open irrevocable documentary acceptance credits in their favour at their foreign bank. Their London branch takes the bills for current shipments on the security of the shipping documents. When accepted they can be discounted.

Importers can also arrange acceptance credits with acceptance houses or banks who accept bills drawn on them subject to conditions, but again they may require partial cash cover. The proceeds then go to the bank's overseas agents who pay the supplier when he hands over the shipping documents. Alternatively, an overseas supplier may arrange with a London bank to draw bills on the security of the shipping documents, which are released to you against payment. They may have a documentary credit with a London bank to negotiate bills drawn by you on them. The bills are presented to the London branch which sends them to the overseas customer's bank where they are surrendered for cash or against acceptance of the bills.

Overseas suppliers can also draw sight or time bills on UK customers. Sight bills are sent to the UK with the shipping documents and presented to the importer for payment against delivery of the documents. With time bills the importer arranges a credit with a foreign branch or correspondent of his bank who buys it at the bank's buying rate of exchange for similar UK drafts. The importer accepts it on D/A terms (documents against acceptance) when the goods are delivered on arrival or are warehoused and insured at the importer's expense until the bill is paid at maturity, although he may be able to take earlier delivery by paying a premium.

Acceptance credits are often made on a revolving basis: when drafts mature, new drafts are drawn up to an agreed maximum. Raw materials are sometimes bought through London acceptance houses by acceptance credit. Drafts are accepted up to a specified amount drawn on the bank by a manufacturer, usually payable three months after date. The manufacturer must put the bank in funds at or before maturity date by way of cash or bills which can be discounted when accepted.

The Export Credits Guarantee Department (ECGD) offers credit insurance by way of guarantees direct to exporters and on goods and services sold on credit terms to the financing bank.

Different arrangements apply to ECGD support for UK exports to the EU and unconditional guarantees are available.

Cover on loans through foreign banks can also be arranged through the ECGD. Information and advice is available from your own bank and the government services, including the DTI.

Information about insurance for importers on credit purchases is obtainable through the DTI. Similar schemes to the ECGD's are available if you are buying abroad and buyer credit guarantees from the supplying country may be available.

Selling debts

You can sell debts for cash under a factoring agreement, which sets out your undertakings as to the status of the debts, the factor's rights and the price paid for advance payment. The factor acts as a collection agent and is responsible for keeping accounts. You usually receive immediate payment of up to 80 per cent of the invoices accepted and the balance when the debt is paid, less the factor's charges, usually between 0.75 to 2.5 per cent of turnover. The initial lump sum payment will also be discounted at a rate similar to bank charges on secured overdrafts, plus a flat monthly fee or a percentage of turnover. The agreement may attract stamp duty and should be registered as an assignment of book debts under the Bills of Sale Act or the Companies Act. Some banks offer a factoring service, buying debts at a discount on the security of invoices and interest is charged on the payment at a rate that is usually about the same as bank interest charged on secured overdraft facilities. You receive the balance of the face value of the invoice when the debt is paid. Other variations are *non-recourse factoring*, swhich provides 100 per cent credit cover on approved debts and *recourse factoring*, which usually provides more cash but no credit protection.

With invoice discounting, you retain control of the sales ledger and chase debts yourself. Again, you receive up to 80 per cent of accepted invoices and the balance less the discounter's charges when the debts are paid and, again, the charge is a discount on the initial lump sum payment plus a flat monthly fee or a percentage of turnover.

Statutory references

Banking Act 1979
Bank of England (Time of Noting) Act 1917
Bills of Exchange Act 1882
Cheques Act 1957 and 1992
Companies Act 1985
Consumer Credit Act 1974
European Communities Act 1972

11

Patents, copyright and trade marks

Goods, services and anything manufactured, marketed or produced which depend for profitability and/or marketability on novelty or brand name is 'intellectual property'. Like any other property, the law protects it.

Protection provided by the law

Protection varies but is principally aimed at stopping competitors exploiting your product or process without consent and covers:

- patent law – protecting 'uniqueness' of technological inventions;
- copyright – protecting literary, artistic and musical works, computer programs and databases, films, recordings, broadcasts and cable programmes;
- design right – protecting the appearance of mass-produced articles;
- trade marks – protecting commercial labels;
- protection against competitors disparaging your products maliciously and 'passing off' their products as yours;
- commercial exploitation of industrial secrets.

Rights are enforced by similar actions but costs vary. Patent actions are the most lengthy, complicated and costly and often cease to be commercially important before trial. Copyright, trade mark and passing off actions can be brought to trial within months and cost far less. Actions for infringing industrial design vary in cost and complexity, depending on the conduct of the action and the approach.

An interlocutory – pre-trial – injunction ordering a defendant not to continue or to embark on a course of action until trial is a fast and relatively cheap route but the plaintiff must in return undertake to compensate the defendant if the case is lost. If the plaintiff then wins, he can obtain a continuing injunction, delivery up or destruction of infringing items and compensation for financial loss. Trade mark owners may also claim advertising costs for restoring their position, copyright and patent owners can claim compensation for forced reductions in price pending trial, and plaintiffs in passing off and slander of goods actions can claim compensation for damage to goodwill. Copyright owners can also claim damages for conversion, ie for work sold, or destroyed by, or as a result of, infringement.

It is proposed to introduce voluntary Alternative Dispute Resolution (ADR) in the Patents County Courts to provide low cost handling of intellectual property disputes to be heard by specialist single arbitrators whose award or decision will be binding. Mediation is part of the package which should offer a fast and relatively cheap route to a legally enforceable settlement.

Patents

Patent law gives temporary protection to unique articles and manufacturing processes superior to their predecessors and a properly drawn up patent gives a complete monopoly. Novelty is the basis of a patent and the product's importance decides whether competitors risk legal action or try to avoid your monopoly. The length of the protection may be decisive as to the practicability of competitors doing the necessary work to sidestep your patent.

Patent protection abroad is obtained through national applications in each country or under the European Patent Convention (EPC). A single EPC application through the London Patent Office or the EU Patent Office in Munich grants a bundle of national patents. Enforcement and validity are determined by national law so results may not be consistent. Most but not all of the EU is covered and eventually there will be a single patent enforceable throughout the EU.

Agreements restricting competition

The following agreements should be drafted by specialists to ensure compliance with both British and EU law.

Patent licences

The manufacture, import, sale and use of patented articles or processes is only lawful with the consent of the patent holder, and with important exceptions you can agree any terms. When you license manufacture, it is implied you can use and sell the product/process yourself. Anyone knowing of restrictions must comply with them or risk infringement but not every restriction is lawful. Under EU law you cannot limit inter-product competition which precludes granting an exclusive licence but there are some block exemptions. British law is also restrictive and you cannot usually force a licensee to buy unpatented materials, although you can agree preferential terms on unpatented goods if you comply with EU law.

Know-how licensing

These also restrict competition in breach of both British and EU law but there are individual and block exemptions.

Research and development

Cooperation agreements for research and development are usually permitted under EU law and, although conditions are strictly defined, some agreements are specifically exempt.

Copyright

Copyright, design right and computer programs are protected under copyright law. Most industrial designs are copyright through initial drawings or prototype models, and copyright exists as soon as pen is put to paper or the model takes shape without registration or legal formalities. There is no copyright in an idea and others with the same idea have their own copyright but your copyright stops exact copying.

Copyright gives the owner the right to stop others from doing something.

If recorded in writing (ie in notation or code, by hand or otherwise) copyright covers:

- original literary, dramatic works (including dance or mime) – no aesthetic merit or style is required, so lists, catalogues, etc are included;
- computer programs, databases and software products;
- original musical works – ie music excluding words or action;
- part or all the typographical arrangements of published editions of literary, dramatic and musical works;
- original artistic works comprising graphics (photographs, sculptures or collages irrespective of artistic quality), architecture (buildings or models for buildings) and works of artistic craftsmanship;
- original sound recordings, films, broadcasts, teletext, satellite and cable programmes.

The 'author' is usually the first owner. Otherwise the first owner is:

- the creator of literary, dramatic, musical and artistic works;
- the person responsible for undertaking arrangements for making computer programs;
- the person undertaking arrangements for making original sound recordings, films and cable programmes;
- the person making broadcasts;
- the employer for work done in the course of employment but the creator may retain moral rights *and* the publisher is the owner of published works.

Both 'author' and country of first publication must qualify for protection. Broadly, protection covers British citizens, subjects and nationals, citizens of British dependent territories, British protected persons domiciled or resident in the UK and in countries covered by the Act and companies incorporated under British law for 70 years. For design right protection, qualifying countries extend to cover member states of the EU.

'Premier league' electronic and paper database creators are protected for the life of the 'author' plus 70 years whether or not the database is innovative. For 'first league' databases the period is life plus 15 years. 'Premier league' databases, eg *Yellow Pages*, indicate by their complex structure that some 'intellectual creativity' was involved, while 'first league' databases, eg telephone directories, are compiled through a basic mechanical arrangement of information. But the dividing line is unclear. Records of how a database was created using intellectual effort could help in obtaining maximum protection and unless created by employees, you should require creators to assign copyright to you or the business.

These apply to all and a substantial part of the works and there is infringement if any of the following are done without the owner's consent:

- copying, ie making a facsimile copy, including reduction or enlargement;
- issuing copies to the public, including renting out sound recordings, films and computer programs – but only when first issued;
- publicly performing literary and dramatic works, including audio and visual representations and publicly playing and showing recordings, films, broadcasts and cable programmes;
- broadcasting or including the work in cable service;
- adapting and translating literary, dramatic and musical works, and doing any of the above in relation to an adaptation.

Permitted acts include:

- 'fair dealing' with a substantial part of a work – this allows use compatible with fair practice and justified in the circumstances, eg for criticism and reporting, *but* copying of literary, dramatic, musical and artistic works is only permitted for private study, research or educational purposes *and* reprographic copying and copying some public documents is restricted;

- performing, playing and showing works for educational purposes;
- copying works in electronic form if purchased on terms that permit it;
- rental of computer programs 70 years from the end of the year of first public issue;
- 'reasonable extracts' of public readings in sound recordings, broadcasts or cable programmes unless expressly prohibited;
- copying works other than broadcasts, cable programmes and typographical arrangements for use within 28 days by broadcasters and cable programme operators.

'Authors' of literary, dramatic, musical and artistic works and film directors have moral rights personal to them which cannot be assigned. Rights extend to adaptations and false attribution and essentially give rights to be given credit and have the creation respected. They cover:

- harm to reputation;
- 'paternity right' – to be identified (*but* not for computer programs or typeface design);
- 'right of integrity' – to object to derogatory treatment, ie additions, alterations and adaptations other than translation or change of musical key or register if there is distortion or mutilation, or honour or reputation is prejudiced (*but* computer programs and reports of current events are excluded);
- right to privacy of some photographs and films;
- the right not to have the work changed and possibly to have it maintained in good condition;
- exclusive right to authorise publication;
- right to withdraw and revise the work.

An employer owning copyright has no moral rights and they do not apply to fair dealing and incidental inclusion in sound recordings, films, broadcasts or cable programmes.

Rights are infringed by possession, sale, hire, rental or exhibition in the course of business or distribution which affects the author or director's honour or reputation.

Rights can be assigned in writing but only exclusive licences must be in writing. You can assign future rights and assignments for part of the copyright period.

The owner and exclusive licensee can stop infringement by injunction and obtain:

- search warrants and orders for delivery up and seizure of infringing copies – in some circumstances owners can seize copies themselves;
- accounts of profits;
- damages – *but* not if the infringer did not know or had no reason to believe copyright subsisted;
- an order restraining 'derogatory' treatment of moral rights of an author or director.

Devices for copy protection (software preventing unauthorised copying or use) are protected if the infringer knows or has reason to believe they are used for making infringing copies. They may also be protected under unfair competition law.

Broadly, these cover 'dealing', including importing and exhibiting, when the defendant knows or has reason to believe the articles are infringing copies and the 'consent or connivance' of a company's officers brings liability on them as well as the company.

Offences punishable with a fine and/or imprisonment are:

- playing or showing infringing works *but* not receiving infringing broadcasts or cable progammes unless intending to avoid payment;
- making or possessing articles designed or adapted for copying, knowing or having reasonable cause to believe they will be used to make infringing copies for sale, hire or use in business;
- gaining unauthorised access to a computer system;
- carrying out unauthorised modifications to, or erasing, a computer program.

The criminal courts can order search and seizure of infringing copies and Customs and Excise will stop imports at the owner's request.

Data protection

If you store data about living individuals who can be identified from your filing system or accessible records, you must register with the Data Protection Commissioner under the 1998 Data Protection Act. Forms and information are available from the Office of the Data Protection Registrar and an annual licence costs £35. Failure to comply with the Act can lead to prosecution, refusal of registration or service of enforcement transfer prohibition, or deregistration notices.

If requested, you must give data subjects details of the information stored, including its sources, uses, why it is held and to whom it is disclosed. You can charge a fee for the service. You can be required to cease processing the data if it is causing or is likely to cause unwarranted and substantial damage to the data subject or anyone else, and the data subject can apply to court for compensation. If the data is incorrect or misleading, you can be required to rectify, block, erase or destroy it, and the data subject can refer to the Commissioner to assess whether you are contravening the Act.

Non-disclosure of some data is permitted, including management forecasts, management planning and information relating to national security, crime, taxation, health, education and social work.

Rights last 70 years from the end of the calendar year of the performance. Infringement is by recording, live transmission and possessing, using, importing and dealing in illicit recordings. Performers and those with whom they have exclusive contracts can consent to breach of copyright – even though the performer is in breach of contract – or sue for infringement. The court can order search, seizure, delivery up and destruction of recordings, films and equipment adapted to produce them and it is a criminal offence to make, deal with or use illicit recordings. Defences are similar to those in other criminal copyright proceedings and penalties include fines and/or imprisonment.

Design right

'Design right' gives the following periods of protection to registered designs and artistic works:

- original non-commonplace designs of an article's shape or configuration – 10 years from first marketing with a 15-year limit from creation;
- registered designs – a maximum of 25 years;
- articles designed as artistic works exploited industrially – 25 years;
- artistic works not exploited industrially – 50 years.

There can be partial transmission of some rights and of part of the protected period. Assignments must be in writing and, unless otherwise agreed, registered design right includes design right.

Rights are slightly different from copyrights.

- Primary right is an exclusive right to reproduce commercially. There is primary infringement when articles are copied 'exactly or substantially to' the design. 'Kits' – 'complete or substantially complete' sets of component parts which infringe when made up are included.
- Importing, possessing for commercial purposes, or dealing commercially with an infringing article knowing or having reason to believe it is such is secondary infringement.

There is a limited defence too of innocence and if the design is copyright and copyright is not infringed, there is no infringement of design right.

During the last five years of protection there is a 'licence of right' to perform restricted acts.

Design right owners and exclusive licensees have the same remedies as copyright owners and the court can also order forfeiture, destruction or other disposal of infringing articles. Unlike copyright, design right is effective only in the UK.

Non-functional designs, ie shapes, configurations or ornaments with eye appeal, applied to articles by an industrial process are protected by registration. The test of infringement is the eye of a customer interested in design. Registration is expensive but worthwhile if the design is an almost inevitable development in its field. It is then infringed by anyone using it, even if created entirely without reference to the design. The author is the original owner but the commissioner and employer are owners of commissioned designs and designs made in the course of employment.

The owner has exclusive rights to make, import for sale, hire or use for the purposes of trade and to sell, hire, offer or expose for sale or hire articles for which the design is registered and to which it, or one not substantially different, has been applied. Infringement is doing any of these without consent and making anything, or enabling anything to be made, to which the design is applied. Rights last for five years, extendable by five-year periods to a maximum of 25 years. There is a six months' grace period at the end of each period to permit late application and rights can be restored if registration lapses.

It is proposed to introduce a community design system including a registered element to be administered by the Office for the Harmonization of the Internal Market in Alicante.

Confidential information

Information, including trade and technological secrets, commercial records and marketing, professional and managerial procedures, can be protected by obtaining undertakings to keep it confidential. This is only possible with those who receive information directly or indirectly and the law is reluctant to impose obligations on ex-employees to stop them using their knowledge and skill.

Domain names

A domain name – your label on the Internet – protects your business name from 'cybersquatters'. Check the availability of the name online at registration agents' or authorities' sites, such as www.netnames.co.uk or www.nominet.com. There is usually no charge and you do not need to establish a Web site to register a domain name.

Trade marks

Trade marks are defined as signs capable of being represented graphically and which distinguish your goods or services. They can be words, names, designs, letters, numerals, the shape of goods or packaging, or distinctive sounds or smells, provided they can be graphically represented. Collective marks which distinguish goods and services of members of an association are also protected. A trade mark search shows existing and pending registrations, but the search is technical and you are advised to use a trade mark agent. Details can be found at www.itma.org.uk, www.cipa.org.uk or www.patent.gov.uk. The agent can also check for rights of reputation or 'passing off' rights (see below).

Registration is refused if the mark:

- is not distinctive;
- consists of signs or indications designating the goods' or services' characteristics, eg quality, quantity, purpose, geographical origin, *unless* the mark is distinctive through use;
- is already established in the trade or in use;
- is likely to be confused with existing marks – *but* the owner of an earlier mark can consent to registration *and* if the applicant shows 'honest concurrent use', registration is allowed.

Registration is for ten years, renewable for further ten-year periods.

When the mark is registered the owner can prevent the use of:

- an identical mark for identical and similar goods/services;
- a similar mark for similar or identical goods/services if there is a likelihood of confusion;
- an identical or similar mark for non-similar goods/services where the infringer would take unfair advantage of or damage the owner's established reputation.

And the owner can require infringing articles to be handed over and claim damages.

If the mark is well known but unregistered, the owner can stop use of a similar or identical mark for similar or identical goods/services and require infringing articles to be handed over but cannot claim damages.

Service marks identify services and are registered and protected in the same way as trademarks.

Applications are made in the member states and rights are enforceable against imports from outside the EU. Owners in an EU member state can, however, only stop imports of goods with the same mark from another member state if they were wrongfully marketed in the exporting state by the exporter or marketed without the owner's consent in the importing country and there must be no link between the two owners. The owner cannot stop marked goods sold in the EU from being resold, even if the marks in member states have different owners.

This is an alternative to a national mark available in 1996 from the Community Trade Mark Office in Alicante, Spain. The mark must be distinctive and the name must not mislead, or be contrary to EU public policy, or already be in use within the EU.

Registration will give EU protection and the owner will be able to stop imitation or use of the mark for similar goods and services or exploitation of its commercial value, but infringement proceedings will be governed by national law. Rights are transferable and can be licensed. Registration is for ten years, renewable for a further ten years but the owner must put the CTM to genuine use in the EU during the first five years.

The EU mark will eventually link into the world intellectual property system with headquarters in Geneva through which protection can be obtained in about 30 countries. The mark is circulated but it is processed in accordance with national laws and the applicant receives national registrations.

Certification trade marks

These show that the owner's goods have reached a certified standard. Certification requires compliance with standards and use approved by the Department of Trade and Industry, details of which are obtainable from the Patent Office. Owners are usually trade or similar organisations and often manufacturers are authorised to apply the mark under the owner's supervision. The mark is not registered and ownership can only be transferred with the consent of the DTI.

Passing off

Passing off covers everything from dishonest trading to near infringement of trade marks, but actions are often concerned with business names because registration of a name gives no right to exclusive use. Most actions involve applying a distinctive badge, sign, label or distinctive package or appearance to goods, thereby implying they are someone else's. The badge must be something used by another trader which deceives, misleads or confuses the customer. There must be a real likelihood of financial loss and it is irrelevant whether other traders or the general public are misled and whether the deception is a mistake, an accident or fraudulent. You are entitled to compensation and an order forbidding continuance of the deception, but full trials are rare because of the difficulty of proving deception.

Slander of goods

This is also called slander of title, trade libel and injurious falsehood and consists of injury to someone's business by making a false and derogatory statement to a third party for an indirect or dishonest motive. The statement must be false and actual, or a genuine risk of financial loss must be proved.

Restrictive trade practices

Producers and suppliers of goods and services must register agreements where at least two parties restrict their conduct in one or more of the ways listed in the Competition Act 1998. The Act is concerned with unfair competition, particularly with terms relating to:

- prices and charges;
- terms and conditions of supply;
- quantities, descriptions and areas for the supply of goods and services;
- to and by whom goods and services are supplied;
- manufacturing processes.

For instance, it is unlawful – as being against the public interest – for manufacturers or suppliers exclusively to tie traders to one dealer for spares.

Patent, registered design and copyright licences are not registrable if the only restrictions concern the invention, the article for which the design is registered, or the copyright. But again, it must be registered if at least two parties accept restrictions.

Exchange of information agreements may be exempt if they relate to manufacturing processes. Trademark licences may be exempt if restrictions relate only to goods bearing the mark or to manufacturing processes. Once registered, agreements can only be modified through the Restrictive Trade Practices Court or the Director of Fair Trading. If they are not price-fixing agreements the Director can state they are 'non-notifiable' and will not refer them to the Restrictive Trade Practices Court. He also has a discretion to accept undertakings from monopoly traders involved in anti-competitive practices.

The system is to be replaced by a general prohibition on agreements and concerted practices which have or may have the object or effect of preventing, restricting or distorting competition. The wording is similar to provisions in EU law rendering such agreements illegal.

The Office of Fair Trading supplies information about registrable agreements and further information may be available from your trade association.

This is, however, a complicated area, and if your contracts are likely to be affected, you should take legal advice.

Statutory references

Competition Act 1980 & 1998
Computer Misuse Act 1990
Consumer Credit Act 1974
Copyright, Designs and Patents Act 1988
Criminal Damage Act 1971
Data Protection Act 1988
Defamation Act 1952
Deregulation and Contracting Out Act 1994
Design Copyrights Act 1968
European Communities Act 1972
Fair Trading Act 1973
Patents Act 1977
Patents (Amendment) Act 1978
Patents, Designs and Marks Act 1986

Registered Designs Act 1949
Trade Descriptions Acts 1968 and 1972
Trade Marks Act 1994
Video Recordings Act 1984 and 1993

12 *Debt collection and litigation*

Delayed payment has a disastrous impact on profits, especially if interest rates are high. Effective credit control backed up by efficient debt collection with a prompt resort to law can help.

Records

Your customer lists should record full names and addresses of the businesses and proprietors. Credit should be given personally to the proprietors of businesses using a trading name.

Terms and conditions of business

Terms and conditions, including interest on delayed payments, should be included in quotations, estimates, acknowledgements of orders, invoices and delivery notes. They can include a right to retain title to goods until payment, but the term should be professionally drawn. They should be legible and intelligible. If referred to court, you will have to show they have been understood, particularly if dealing with consumers. In dealing with businesses – but not consumers – a separate agreement confirming acceptance of your terms and conditions is useful.

You can now claim (statutory) interest at 8 per cent above current bank base rate on debts for goods and services where both you and your buyer or supplier are acting in the course of business. Interest becomes due on the day after the specified date for payment, the 30th day after delivery of the goods or services or the 30th day after the purchaser is notified of the amount owed – whichever is the later.

A term excluding statutory interest is void unless you have agreed an alternative remedy for late payment that is reasonable in the context of the contract.

Internal procedures

Limits should be put on credit. Cheques should be backed by banker's cards and the number written on the back of the cheque by the payee. Most cards guarantee payment of £50 to £100 and the cheque must cover only one invoice up to the stated limit, otherwise the bank can refuse to honour the cheque. For a fee, your bank will expedite presentation of cheques to the payer's bank. Payment by credit card is a contract, with the card holder as the card company's agent – if the card company becomes insolvent, you cannot sue the card holder.

Weekly or monthly balances should be kept on running accounts, with a cut-off point for legal proceedings. Small amounts should be paid promptly on delivery, preferably by cash or cheque – even post-dated. Acceptance of part payment in 'full and final settlement' does not debar further demands or court proceedings for the balance unless the debtor has given fresh consideration – ie done something to his or her detriment not called for under your agreement – in return for your agreement to take no further action.

Your best cover is a personal guarantee from the debtor and, if the amount is substantial, a third party, but before allowing a substantial debt to accrue or suing a debtor, it is worthwhile carrying out checks through searches at:

- Companies House;
- The Land Charges and Land Registry;

- The Registers of:
  - Bills of Sale;
  - Bankruptcy Petitions and Orders;
  - Deeds and Arrangements;
  - County Court Judgments;

  but registration is against an address, not an individual, so check the entries actually relate to your debtor;
- Hire Purchase Information Limited and other credit information services and credit references agencies.

When legal action is inevitable, letters of demand should be worded carefully, setting a time limit for payment. Before issuing proceedings, you should deliver a standard 'letter before (legal) action' on which you can take proceedings.

Settling disputes by arbitration

It is worth considering arbitration. It can be flexible, fast and relatively cheap, specifically tailored to fit the dispute and heard by a specialist in the trade. Many trade organisations offer schemes, although some are thought to be biased in favour of their members. Consumers have the right to refer instead to the court, but the commercial court encourages litigants to consider the simpler and faster Alternative Dispute Resolution (ADR) and will, if appropriate, adjourn court proceedings while this is done.

Litigation

Litigation is a last resort, to be taken only if you expect to obtain payment and/or compensation. Commercial litigation is dealt with by the civil courts – the High Court and the County Court. The courts have similar procedure and debt collection is relatively straightforward. Experienced legal practitioners are best equipped to deal with the finer points of High Court pleading and advocacy, and whatever the claim, you may face expensive opposition.

Sole traders, partners and directors earning up to £7,777 pa, with disposable capital of up to £6,750 (£8,571 and £8,560 respectively in personal injury claims) are eligible for legal aid, but not companies, and litigation is expensive. Leading firms charge hourly rates of £750-plus, but unless you have a specialist and substantial claim, you are unlikely to need the constant attention of the most senior partner or a QC. However, even in a fairly straightforward County Court claim, the bill can be several thousand pounds and, win or lose, you pay for work done before litigation.

The Gaming Act forbids some types of betting, but solicitors can now gamble on litigation and you may be able to proceed through a contingency fee. Your lawyers are entitled to a percentage of any winnings and insurance is available, but ensure all the terms of the contingency fee agreement are clearly spelt out. Alternatively, you may be able to obtain insurance cover for the litigation. Your solicitor will be able to give you details.

Your solicitor needs the facts, the documents (including a statement of account), relevant correspondence and details of a possible defence. If you are continuously referring debts to your solicitor, it is worth agreeing a standard referral procedure, with periodic summaries and settlement.

You can, however, litigate in person in any court and the small-claims track procedure in the County Court is specifically designed with this in mind. The emphasis here is therefore on suing in the County Court. If facts are in dispute or the claim is substantial, your best course is to instruct a solicitor.

Criminal proceedings

Crime is the business of the magistrates' and crown courts and the police or responsible authority. It is no crime if debts are not paid or you carry on business at a loss unless fraud is involved. But you can be prosecuted under health and safety consumer protection, licensing, and road traffic legislation.

If you are prosecuted, whatever the circumstances, you need legal advice. Conviction can have serious repercussions in civil proceedings for compensation – conviction for a minor traffic offence linked to injury or property damage is automatically admissible, and negligence thereby proved in civil proceedings.

A prosecution in the magistrates' court is based on information stating that someone has, or is suspected of having, committed an offence. A summons or warrant to arrest is issued requiring the accused to appear in court. Warrants can only be obtained in specific circumstances, including for offences punishable with imprisonment and/or triable by jury.

More serious offences are heard in the Crown Court before a jury. The Crown Court also hears appeals from some civil decisions made in the Magistrates' courts, eg decisions concerning licensing and recovery of unpaid income tax and NICs.

In police and in private prosecutions, an innocent party's costs may be paid if the accused is clearly innocent. But, as in any other litigation (unless there is full legal aid), innocent defendants pay part of the costs.

Civil actions

The High Court and the County Court deal with contractual, property and partnership disputes, business tenancies and tort claims. Contractual claims cover disputes about written or unwritten agreements. Claims in tort include claims in negligence, eg for compensation for injury or property damage caused in an accident. Straightforward cases are usually dealt with in the County Court. The High Court deals with more challenging cases and claims involving more substantial damages, professional negligence, fatal accidents, allegations of fraud or undue influence, defamation, malicious prosecution or false imprisonment and claims against the police.

The County Court office will help you to deal with forms and issue proceedings. District judges are used in cases involving up to £5,000, while more important or complex cases involving more than £5,000 are usually heard by a circuit judge.

Court fees are additional to legal costs. You pay between £20 and £400 to start an action, depending on the amount and nature of the claim. The loser pays the fixed costs of taking the action, which vary from £30.75 to £82.00 with the amount and the claim. There is a fee of up to £300 for setting the case down for trial and between £25 and £80 for applying for judgment. A defendant putting in a counter-claim – a money claim exceeding yours – pays between £20 and £400. The winner pays up to £80 to enforce judgment.

There is now a new system under which the judge is case manager. Management now includes pre-action protocols, which aim to encourage cooperation between the parties at an early stage in an effort to narrow the issues and, if possible, to avoid taking the case to court.

The court is required to encourage and facilitate the use of alternative dispute resolution and can stay proceedings to allow for this either at the parties' request or when it considers this appropriate.

Cases are allocated to one of three tracks, depending on the complexity and amount involved, and the judge must:

- encourage the parties to cooperate;
- identify the issues at an early stage;
- dispose of summary issues that do not require full investigation;
- help the parties to settle all or part of the case;
- fix timetables for the hearing and control the progress of the case;
- consider whether the benefit of a particular method of hearing justifies its cost.

Parties refusing to comply may have their case struck out or face sanctions, including costs sanctions.

The categories are:

- *Small-claim track* for cases of up to £5,000 and cases involving over £5,000 with the parties' consent, claims for personal injury where the amount of damages claimed does not exceed £1,000 and some claims by residential tenants. On allocation, a date is fixed for a preliminary or final hearing and directions for case management ensure the trial proceeds quickly and efficiently. Procedure is aimed at keeping costs to a minimum by dispensing with formalities and is designed for the litigant in person in the cases of debt claims, consumer disputes, accident claims, disputes about ownership of goods and some landlord and tenant disputes.
- *Fast track* for cases involving over £5,000 and less than £15,000. There are standard directions for trial preparation and a maximum of one day (five hours) for trial with, usually, no oral expert evidence and costs are fixed. Claims exceeding £15,000 are also allocated to fast track if the trial is likely to last for only one day and there is only one expert on each side in two areas of expertise.

- *Multi track* for more complex cases and those involving over £15,000. There is no standard procedure and there is a range of case management provisions, including standard directions, conferences and pretrial reviews.

Local County Courts are listed in the telephone directory. You must usually sue in the court closest to where the defendant lives or carries on business, or where the incident on which the claim is based occurred. On a contract, you sue where the contract was concluded. If you choose the wrong court, the case is transferred at extra cost.

Time limits are basic. The court serves the proceedings on the defendant. If there is no response, you can ask for bailiff service or serve proceedings yourself. You must file the other documents in the proceedings with the court and serve them on the defendant yourself. You must therefore ask for acknowledgement of service (receipt) of documents that are 'served' the day following postage to the appropriate address by first-class post.

The claimant starts the action and the person sued is the defendant. It is not usually difficult to identify your opponent unless there are several possibilities, eg in a road accident claim you may want to sue the driver, car owner and/or the driver's employer. Multiple defendants pay in proportion to their liability.

Proceedings must be filed with the court and served on (ie delivered to) the defendant or his or her solicitor.

Service on a limited company is to the registered office on business documents and filed at Companies House. Companies cannot litigate 'in person', but you can apply for an order permitting a director or officer to appear for the company. The Articles may require the consent of the board or the shareholders before proceedings brought by a company can be continued.

The partnership's name and address for service are on business documents and filed at Companies House.

Someone using a trade name can be served by naming him or her or the business as defendant and serving proceedings at his or her principal place of business or residence.

The names of directors and of up to 20 partners are on business documents and filed at Companies House. Partners must disclose their names and addresses to the court, whether sued personally or in the partnership name, and can be served personally or at the principal place of business.

The first step is to complete a claim form with the names and addresses of the parties, concise details of the claim and why you are taking action, and a statement of value together with a statement of truth as to its contents. If you need to set out the facts at length, they must be contained in a separate document – the particulars of claim. If sent separately, it must be filed with the Court Office within 14 days of serving the claim form on the defendant, together with its own statement of truth.

The County Court is not strict about form and in a straightforward claim for debt, 'I claim £X the price of goods sold and delivered to Y on. . .', is sufficient, but usually pleadings refer to claimant *and* defendant: 'the claimant claims £X'. Other claims require more details, eg road accident particulars must list the date, place and circumstances of the accident, say why the defendant was responsible and whether, as a result, you suffered pain, injury, loss or damage. If suing a driver's employer because the driver was working at the time of the accident, you must state that the driver was 'acting in the course of his/her employment'. Expenses and loss of earnings must also be listed; 'The claimant claims damages limited to £X' covers only general compensation assessed by the court. Interest may be awarded if included in the particulars.

A payment in or offer to settle made in writing 'and without prejudice except as to costs' by either party may dispose of the claim. An offer can be made at any time but payment in cannot be made before proceedings have issued. Thereafter, offer or payment in can be made any time before judgment, but, if not accepted, it must not be disclosed to the judge until after judgment but before costs are dealt with. If judgment exceeds the payment, the defendant pays the claimant's costs, but if the he guessed right or judgment is for less, the defendant pays costs to the date of payment and the claimant pays both sides' costs thereafter.

You can apply for summary judgment even if the defendant has filed an acknowledgement of service or a defence. You must file written evidence with the court to support your claim, together with a statement of truth, file it with the court and serve it on the defendant. If no defence is served, you may have to wait until the hearing before you hear whether the defendant admits, defend and/or counterclaims, or whether there is a 'set-off' – eg for storage charges. If there is an arguable defence, the debtor may be permitted to defend on conditions – eg that all or part of the amount is paid into court pending trial. If there is a good defence, no conditions are imposed. If, however, the defendant admits the debt or you obtain judgment, the debt is entered on the Register of County Court Judgments and cancelled if paid within a month. Otherwise it stays on for six years and, when the court is notified of payment, it is noted against the entry.

The defendant may, however, make an offer to pay by instalments. If you reject instalment payments of a debt of less than £50,000, a court officer can decide without a hearing whether or not it should be accepted, taking into account the defendant's statement of means, other relevant information and your objections. If the officer does not make a decision, a judge will do so, with or without a hearing, and either party can apply to have the decision re-determined by a judge.

Judgment may be obtained without the defendant receiving notice of proceedings. The defendant must then immediately ask the court for details, producing the order for judgment. It is set aside if proceedings have not been properly served. Otherwise, it is set aside only if there is a reasonable defence and explanation for non-response and the defendant may have to pay costs to the date of judgment.

If you do not apply for summary judgment, the defence to a disputed claim must be filed with a statement of truth within 14 days. This can be extended to 28 days if the defendant instead files an acknowledgement of service within 14 days and files the defence 14 days thereafter.

Lists of relevant documents and other evidence are then exchanged and made available for inspection, including statements reports, photographs and sketch plans, unless otherwise ordered. 'Without prejudice' oral and written offers of settlement are excluded unless you choose to put them in evidence.

Agreement saves costs. For instance, you may be able to agree the cost of repairs instead of bringing witnesses to trial, leaving only liability for the trial.

The parties can ask for orders permitting them to act, or directing their opponent to do (or stop doing) something, pending the hearing. These applications are interlocutory and are made *inter partes* – on notice to the other side – or, if urgent, *ex parte* – without notice – at fees of between £25 and £50. Usually they must be served and filed, and the court office will tell you about time limits and restrictions. Some interlocutory orders, eg an injunction to stop someone trading, can be expensive because the court may require an undertaking to pay damages accruing until the hearing.

If costs are not agreed between the parties, the court will make 'detailed assessment' of costs at the end of the case. The court can, however, assess them on a summary basis at any stage and ask for estimates of accrued and future costs, and may order a payment on account of costs pending detailed assessment.

Costs are payable within 14 days of judgment unless the court orders otherwise and assessment is on a standard or indemnity basis.

Standard costs are those proportionate to the claim and reasonably incurred in the circumstances. Proportionality is not a factor in awarding costs on an Indemnity basis. Whether standard or indemnity, the court takes into account the parties' conduct, the amount of money or property involved, its importance to the parties, the complexity of the case and the time, skill and specialised knowledge of those involved.

You may be able to appeal against a decision you think is wrong. The court office will inform you of time limits and explain procedures, but before appealing you should take legal advice.

Collecting debts after County Court litigation

When judgment is obtained, you can enlist the court's help in enforcing it by 'warrant'. Judgments requiring money payment (including judgments in the High Court), whatever the amount, registered judgments for debt and damages in the High Court of Scotland and Northern Ireland, or directing the transfer, delivery or recovery of possession of money or property, can be enforced in the County Court. High Court and County Court enforcement procedures are similar, but County Court enforcement is often less successful because the County Court Bailiff's powers are more restricted than the High Court Sheriff's.

Unless stated to the contrary, stay of execution (delaying enforcement) is automatic for 14 days after money judgment is entered. An order to wind up a company stops execution on judgments against it.

A money judgment debtor can be ordered to attend court for examination as to property and means.

Warrants of execution are enforceable against goods. If located in several areas, concurrent warrants can issue in several courts. Costs are usually allowed and you should tell the court if you reach agreement with the debtor or withdraw from possession so the warrant can be suspended. If reissued, your priority is from the date of reissue.

Warrants are to enforce judgments or orders for recovery, or delivery of possession of land, and can issue 14 days after judgment or the day after a defendant is ordered to vacate. The court can suspend orders of possession for arrears of rent or under a mortgage and the warrant is cancelled on payment of arrears plus costs.

Delivery of goods is enforced by warrant of delivery or attachment. On assessed value, you can execute for the value, or judgment may permit retaining goods pending payment. Injunctions and orders are enforced by warrant of attachment.

A judgment debtor may be committed to prison if he or she has persistently and wilfully disobeyed an order. On a money judgment, you must show the debtor had means to pay since judgment.

Charging orders on a debtor's land are made to enforce money judgments. The charge is registrable at the Land Registry or under the Land Charges Act, but not under the Companies Act. Charging orders on company shares and debentures are made on judgments for fixed amounts and can include dividends and interest. You can also obtain a 'stop notice' or injunction, which effectively invalidates dealings.

This is available against anyone in employment, whatever the amount of the debt. You must identify the employer. The debtor must give details of the employment and current and future earnings, resources and needs, and the employer may have to file a statement of the debtor's earnings. The order directs the employer to make deductions from pay and pay them to the court, which must be notified if the employment ends.

Any unconditional debt, even if not immediately payable, can be garnished if it accrues solely to the debtor. Current bank accounts can be attached and (on conditions) deposit accounts, but you may lose priority to a third party if attachment is not completed by payment before a petition for bankruptcy or winding up is lodged.

If you cannot use any other method, the court may agree to appoint a receiver. The order covers the sale proceeds of land or a share of rents and property held jointly or subject to a *lien* or trust. It can include an injunction ancillary or incidental to appointment if the debtor might dispose of the property. The receiver may have to give undertakings to the court or you may be made personally liable for his or her actions. The order does not make you a secured creditor, so it should be registered as a charge or caution if made against land.

Judgment is enforceable against the partnership's and the partners' property and against partners who were served in the proceedings or admitted in the proceedings that they were partners. Charging orders against a partner charge his or her interest in the partnership property, plus the partner's share of profits. By the same or a later order, a receiver can be appointed over other money due to the partner from the partnership and the court can make other orders and directions. The partner or his or her partners can redeem or purchase the charge if a sale is ordered.

The leave of the court is necessary before the partnership or a partner can enforce judgment against another partner.

Enforcement against a company is against the directors or other officers, but leave of the court is required before issue.

Non-compliance with a judgment or order is a ground for bankruptcy or winding up. But service of a statutory demand – which must be for at least £750 – often leads to payment of the amount due without recourse to litigation.

Statutory references

Arbitration Acts 1950, 1975, 1979 & 1996
Attachment of Earnings Act 1971
Civil Procedure Act 1997
Companies Acts 1985 & 1989
Consumer Credit Act 1974
County Courts Act 1984
Courts and Legal Services Act 1990
Criminal Justice Act 1982
Fair Trading Act 1973
Hire Purchase Act 1965
Insolvency Act 1986

Law Reform (Miscellaneous Provisions) Act 1934
Partnership Act 1890
Powers of the Criminal Court Act 1973
Supreme Court Act 1981

13

Bankruptcy and liquidation

Profit patterns fluctuate and projections are not always accurate. Before embarking on the sea of private enterprise, you should have some idea as to what happens if you run aground.

Insolvency

Insolvency is defined as:

- when debts and liabilities – including contingent and prospective – exceed assets;
- failure to pay a judgment debt (resulting from successful legal proceedings);
- failure to pay, compound or secure an undisputed debt of at least £750, within three weeks of formal demand, or if there is a serious possibility assets will be dissipated, forthwith;
- approval of a voluntary arrangement;
- the making of an administrative order;
- the appointment of an administrative receiver.

Only professionally qualified, licensed insolvency practitioners may act in bankruptcies and liquidations.

Extortionate credit bargains (see page 97) may be set aside by the court and onerous (oppressive) contracts for leaseholds can be disclaimed. If not registered under the Bills of Sale or Companies Act, general assignments of book debts are void, unless paid before presentation of a petition, the debts are due under specified contracts or were part of a transfer made in good faith and for value, or the transfer benefited the creditors.

Voidable transactions, preferences and transactions at an undervalue

Sole traders and partnerships

Transactions putting creditors, sureties or guarantors into a better position than other creditors can be set aside as 'preferences', including transactions:

- at an undervalue (ie gifts or transfers made for significantly less than market value or in consideration of marriage) – at risk if made less than five years before presentation of a petition for bankruptcy or an administrative order, *and* if intended to put assets beyond the reach or prejudice the interests of actual or potential creditors;
- at a proper price – at risk for six months but two years if made with an 'associate' (see page 20).

Companies

Voidable periods vary, dating back from presentation of a petition for an administrative order, the date the order is made, or the commencement of liquidation, and:

- transactions at an undervalue are safe if made in good faith, for business purposes and for the company's benefit, *but* are voidable if with a 'connected person' (see page 20);
- preferences made when the company was insolvent or causing insolvency are at risk for six months to two years;
- floating charges are at risk for one or two years.

Trading with an intent to defraud creditors – which may include paying cheques into the company's account after it stops trading – imposes unlimited liability on the directors. In insolvent liquidation directors, *de facto* and shadow directors may be criminally liable and subject to disqualification for wrongful trading. The only defence is that every step was taken to minimise loss.

The voluntary procedures

Insolvent individuals and undischarged bankrupts who have not applied for 12 months, their trustee or the official receiver (a member of staff of the Department of Trade and Industry), can make arrangements with creditors through the court. Partnerships and companies can also agree arrangements and compromises with creditors and apply for administration orders so business can be reorganised and insolvency avoided. An additional voluntary arrangement has been proposed for small companies, allowing them to seek a moratorium (a temporary bar on creditors' claims) to give management time to put together a rescue scheme for the creditors' consideration.

With partnerships, these voluntary arrangements can be used even if an insolvency order is made against the partnership or a partner but there must be interlocking arrangements if the partnership and the partners both want to agree arrangements.

Partners, directors, liquidators or administrators put proposals and a statement of (financial) affairs to creditors – and shareholders – nominating a supervisor. There may be creditors' meetings, secured and preferred creditors are protected as in bankruptcy and liquidation, and on application the court can stay (stop) the proceedings. Disadvantages are that:

- creditors cannot recover VAT bad debt relief;
- until the order is made partners and directors remain at risk.

For companies this is mainly used if there are no standard fixed and floating charges and the court must be satisfied that:

- the business is, or is likely to become, unable to pay its debts;
- all or part of the business would survive as a going concern, and/ or;
- creditors are likely to agree a satisfactory arrangement, and/or;
- realising the assets is likely to be more advantageous than a winding up.

Administration can be in other voluntary arrangements but not if the company is in liquidation.

The partnership and/or the partners or directors and/or creditors can petition. Secured creditors and debenture-holders must be notified and it can only be withdrawn with leave of the court. The administrator takes over management but cannot prevent an application for dissolution or appointment of an administrative receiver (under a company's floating charge). Partners' and directors' powers are restricted, creditors' and shareholders' meetings may be called and a more detailed statement of affairs must be prepared, confirmed on affidavit by current and former partners or directors and in some cases those involved in the company's formation, and employees. The Registrar must be notified and details of the appointment must appear on business documents and in the *Gazette* and in a newspaper that will bring it to the notice of creditors. Creditors and shareholders can apply to court if the business is, was, or will be, managed so they are unfairly prejudiced and the court can regulate the administration.

Administration ends on application to the court either because the purposes specified in the order cannot be carried out or because they have been completed.

Sole trader

Sole traders are personally liable for business debts and obligations. Personal assets, stock in trade and business assets can be sold. All you can keep are tools, books, vehicles and other equipment necessary for personal use in your business or employment and clothing, bedding, furniture and necessary provision for you and your family. But the trustee in bankruptcy can claim items he thinks will sell at more than replacement cost and you may have to pay over part of your earnings until discharge. The trustee, in whom some rights of (legal) action are vested, must be informed of increases in pay and estate (assets) but you can keep property held on trust for others and property payable under third party insurances.

Petitions in bankruptcy, bankruptcy orders and arrangements with creditors are registrable against real property and may bind a purchaser with unregistered title. They can be registered against registered property which stops dealings except through the official receiver or trustee.

Bankruptcy

The petition is presented by the debtor, creditor, supervisor, person acting in, or bound by, a voluntary arrangement, the official receiver, the Director of Public Prosecutions or person named in a Criminal Bankruptcy Order. Issue protects the debtor and his estate from legal proceedings and some legal processes. On a debtor's petition, the court may consider summary administration (for 'small' bankruptcies) and whether there should be a report.

An interim receiver or special manager takes over the debtor's estate pending appointment of a trustee, protecting assets and disposing of those liable to diminish in value. He continues to act in summary administration and criminal bankruptcy.

The debtor is then an undischarged bankrupt, deprived of ownership of most of his assets. He must cooperate with the receiver and hand over books and records. Except on the debtor's petition, a statement of affairs must be provided and there may be public examination in court and creditors' meetings.

Assets available include property acquired before and after the order, assets in voidable transactions and part of current income but the right of occupation of a solvent spouse and dependants is protected. Debts and interest must be proved. Secured creditors can realise or value the security and prove for the balance or surrender it and prove for the full amount. The trustee may continue the business and make periodic payments (dividends).

It is an offence for a bankrupt:

- not to have kept proper accounts for two years prior to the order;
- to have materially contributed to his financial problems by gambling;

- to take assets outside the jurisdiction;
- to make a false statement of affairs;
- to enter into a transaction intending to defraud creditors;
- to go into business in a name other than that stated in the order;
- to act as a director or be involved in company management – anyone acting on the bankrupt's instructions in relation to a company also commits an offence.

And the bankruptcy must be disclosed when applying for credit and accepting payment in advance.

The order of distribution is:

- liquidation costs;
- preferential debts proportionately, ie 12 months' PAYE and NICs, contributions relating to subcontractors in the construction industry, six months' VAT, betting duty, pension scheme contributions, 12 weeks' wage arrears if no notice given, otherwise six weeks, to a maximum of £205, and payments under the employment legislation;
- secured creditors;
- unsecured creditors plus interest until distribution;
- provable debts plus interest due to the bankrupt's spouse.

Bankruptcy dates from the order and lasts until discharge but may be annulled if debts are paid off or secured. Discharge is automatic after three years for the first-time bankrupt, two years in summary administration. Otherwise it can be deferred for up to 15 years. The bankrupt can then go into business and, with some exceptions, is no longer liable for provable debts.

It is proposed that the period of disqualification be extended to 15 years if there was fraud or recklessness, and that if fraudsters seek a loan of more than £250 they will be required to tell the lender they are bankrupt, as well as their business contacts if they go into business under a new name.

Partnerships

Partners have complete financial commitment but commitment to co-partners ends by mutual agreement, dissolution, death and bankruptcy.

Dissolution by agreement is seldom straightforward and the agreement should set out terms applying to dissolution.

The partnership ends if business becomes illegal and unless the agreement states otherwise:

- on completion of the undertaking or end of the period for which it was formed;
- on a partner's bankruptcy, death, or resignation;
- if a partner's share is charged by the court for personal debt – but the other partners can buy it and continue in business.

You can rescind (cancel) the agreement if there is fraud by a potential partner. You are entitled to damages for deceit, a lien (right of retention for the price) on surplus assets equal to your capital contribution, plus interest and costs, an indemnity against partnership debts and repayment of anything paid towards liabilities, plus interest.

Payment for a retiring or deceased partner's share substitutes the agreement to pay for the final account and distribution of assets but you should agree a formal settlement. (An option to purchase limits liability by the terms of the option.) Executors of deceased partners should ask the court to appoint a manager or receiver.

If losses are due to a partner, you can apply to the court – or, with an arbitration clause, the arbitrator – for dissolution on the ground that it is 'just and equitable'.

The court appoints a receiver or receiver and manager who is usually required to take the 'usual accounts and enquiries' and complete the dissolution. Receivers take in income and pay outgoings. Managers continue the business so receivers are usually appointed if the business is to be wound up.

Partners' responsibilities continue until winding up is concluded but only solvent or surviving partners are committed. When surviving partners of a deceased partner mortgage land, the deceased partner's estate may lose priority and the personal representatives should join in conveyances of land bought before 1926. If a partner is bankrupt, his trustee should be a party.

On dissolution, one partner sues in the partnership's name and gets in and distributes the assets. Goodwill must be sold unless otherwise agreed or it is personal and stays with the partners. If sold, they cannot solicit new business with existing connections. Except with a fixed-term partnership terminated by death, repayment of premiums can be ordered and when the assets are sold and the partnership dissolved a general account is made up in accordance with the partnership's usual practice.

Payments go first to preferential then secured creditors and then to pay other debts and liabilities. If there are insufficient partnership assets to pay off creditors, the shortfall ranks with the ordinary debts of the individual partners. Partners' advances come next, then winding up costs and initial capital contributions. If costs are not covered, they are paid proportionately by the partners. Losses, unless otherwise agreed, including capital losses, come from profits, then capital and then from the partners in accordance with their entitlement to share profits.

Insolvency

The law applying to sole traders applies with modifications to partners and partnerships. Regulations have yet to be made concerning insolvency and winding up in limited liability partnerships.

A petition served on a partner is served on the partnership which can be wound up without involving their insolvency but the adjudication order is made against the partners, not the partnership.

The partners (but not a limited partner), creditors or person acting in a voluntary arrangement can petition and the business is wound up as an unregistered company.

Partners, former partners and anyone who has or has had control or management is a director or officer under the insolvency and company directors' disqualification legislation with the liability of directors and management of a limited company.

If one or more partners as well as the partnership is insolvent there are two claims: first, between the partnership's and the partners' creditors if all partners are bankrupt; second, between a bankrupt partner's creditors and solvent co-partners.

If all the partners are bankrupt, creditors can claim against partnership assets and any unpaid balance comes from the partners' estates. Preferred creditors then rank with unsecured creditors but regain priority if payment is made into the joint estate from a partner's estate. Secured creditors can claim against the partnership or a partner without valuing the security. There are the following variations.

- If there are no partnership assets creditors can claim equally from each partner.
- Partners and the partnership are liable for their own fraudulent acts.
- Debts owed by the partnership and the partners can be claimed against the partnership and the partners.
- Creditors who put a partner into bankruptcy can usually also claim as partnership creditors.
- The trustees in bankruptcy of partners in business on their own account can claim against the partnership.
- Partnership creditors have priority over creditors of an insolvent corporate partner; the claims rank *pan passa* (proportionately) between themselves.

Companies

Receivership is when assets secured by a floating charge are realised and paid to the holder. Secured creditors can enforce the security without a winding up and without regard to anyone else's interests.

Outside investors' tax reliefs under the Enterprise Investment Scheme (EIS) or Venture Capital Trust (VCT) scheme are not put at risk if, except for the actions of the receiver, the company still qualifies under the schemes.

Administrative receivers are appointed by debenture-holders or the court in accordance with the debenture. Their powers are similar to those administrators. Floating charges usually include a charge over plant and machinery which may also be covered by a fixed charge. If the company is in default before a winding up resolution, the charge becomes fixed, giving the lender priority over all the creditors. Notice of the appointment must be given to the company and creditors, and appear on company documents, in the *Gazette* and in a newspaper which will bring it to the creditors' notice. The administrative receiver prepares the fuller statement of affairs required in administration and reports to the Registrar and – unless he or she reports within three months – to secured creditors and their trustees and, if appointed, the liquidator. The appointment ends by court order or resignation.

Receivers are appointed under a fixed charge or by the court. They report to directors, shadow directors and the Registrar. If an administrator is appointed the security cannot be enforced without consent of the court or administrator but the fixed chargeholders retain priority if the security is sold. The appointment ends when the receiver has sufficient to pay his expenses and discharge the debt.

Voluntary liquidation

A shareholders' voluntary liquidation is where a majority of the directors produce a satisfactory declaration of solvency, setting out assets and liabilities and stating debts will be paid within 12 months. The shareholders appoint a liquidator and the declaration is filed with the Registrar. If debts are not paid, the directors may be liable to a fine or imprisonment. Pending appointment of a liquidator, the directors cannot, without the consent of the court, do anything except what is necessary to protect company assets. Although the liquidator is not appointed or supervised by creditors most of his powers can only be exercised with the consent of the court until the creditors' meeting.

If there is no declaration, the liquidator disagrees with it or the debts are not paid, it becomes a creditors' voluntary liquidation. Creditors and shareholders nominate liquidators but the creditors' choice takes precedence. A creditors' committee which includes shareholders' representatives may also be appointed to supervise the liquidator. Directors, shareholders and creditors can nominate a joint or alternate liquidator through the court.

The liquidator realises the assets and distributes the proceeds but may need the consent of the court or the creditors' committee.

Outside investors' tax reliefs under the EIS or VCT Schemes are not put at risk in a liquidation.

Liquidation starts with the date of the winding up resolution and lasts until the liquidator vacates office after his final report to shareholders and creditors, but he can resign on notice to the Registrar of the final meeting.

All debts, present, future, certain and contingent, including quantified claims for damages, are provable unless the company is insolvent. Shareholders are only liable for the unpaid balance on their shares. The first payment is under fixed charges, then liquidation expenses, preferential debts, floating charges and arrears of dividends, with remaining assets going equally to unsecured creditors.

The company is dissolved three months from registration by the Registrar of the liquidator's final account and return.

Compulsory winding up

The company, contributories (ie shareholders who have held shares since incorporation or for 6 of the 18 months before liquidation), creditors, the official receiver or the Department of Trade and Industry can lodge the petition.

The court orders compulsory liquidation if:

- the company has not started trading within a year of incorporation or has stopped trading for 12 months;
- the company is insolvent;
- a special resolution requests it;
- it is 'just and equitable' to do so;
- the DTI requests it;
- a director or seller of shares to the company for capital requests it on the ground that it cannot pay its debts or it is just and equitable to do so;
- the company is not pursuing the business activities set out in its Memorandum;
- there is mismanagement or deadlock on the board but this applies only if the court is satisfied that voluntary liquidation is not in the interest of creditors or shareholders.

On making the order the directors' powers cease and the official receiver or provisional liquidator is appointed pending appointment of the liquidator. Details must appear on company documents, be notified to the Registrar and be advertised in the *Gazette* and two local newspapers.

Liquidation starts from presentation of the petition unless there was a voluntary liquidation, when it dates from the date of the resolution. A full statement of affairs may be required and no proceedings can be taken by or against the company without the consent of the court. There may be creditors' and shareholders' meetings. Appointment of the liquidator is as in a creditors' winding up but the official receiver can apply for appointment and creditors and contributories may appoint a liquidation committee. The liquidator realises and distributes the assets and must keep the official receiver informed. The official receiver may report to the court and apply for public examination of anyone involved in the company's affairs. The court can also order examination of company officers.

Penalties

Anyone involved in trading with an intent to defraud, incurring debts without a reasonable prospect of repayment, or convicted for an indictable offence (serious and triable by jury) relating to the company or its assets may be prosecuted and disqualified from participating directly or indirectly in the management of a company for up to 15 years. Gross incompetence and 'commercial immorality' (including failure to carry out statutory duties) also brings disqualification.

If the company bought shares within a year of the winding up and cannot meet debts and liabilities, management may share liability for loss with the holder of the shares.

Directors and shadow directors cannot, without court consent within 12 months of insolvent liquidation act for, or be involved in the promotion, formation or management of, or be connected with, a company with the same name, or use a former name or trading name used during the previous 12 months, or one which suggests continuing association for five years.

Distribution is as in a voluntary liquidation except charges over distrained goods are paid after floating charges.

The official receiver can apply for early dissolution if expenses will not be paid. Otherwise the liquidator reports to creditors and the company is dissolved three months after dissolution is registered.

Statutory references

Attachment of Earnings Act 1971
Bills of Sale Act 1878
Companies Acts 1985 and 1989
Company Directors Disqualification Act 1986

Employment Protection (Consolidation) Act 1978
Insolvency Act 1986
Insolvency Act (No. 2)1994
Land Charges Act 1972
Land Registration Act 1925
Limited Liability Partnership Act 2000
Limited Partnership Act 1907
Matrimonial Homes Act 1983
Partnership Act 1890
Powers of Criminal Courts Act 1973

14 *Takeovers and mergers*

Business is good, profits are climbing, management is efficient – now is the time to consider expansion. But you may also be taking on:

- outstanding and transferred liability for VAT;
- employees' accrued rights on unfair dismissal and redundancy.

If the first move on acquisition is to rationalise by dismissing employees, dismissal is automatically unfair if the reason or principal reason is the takeover. But you can fairly dismiss for 'an economic, technical or organisational reason entailing changes in the workforce'. Even on fair dismissal, there may be entitlement to redundancy payments. You should therefore obtain an indemnity from your seller to cover any claim which might arise on transfer of the business.

The sole trader and expansion

The route to expansion is by way of taking on investors, partners or incorporating yourself as a limited company.

Partnership mergers

When taking on additional partners or amalgamating with another firm, you must change the partnership name and the partnership agreement should be amended to reflect your extended liability for new partners. Existing and incoming partners should elect for continuance, thereby avoiding assessment to tax on the basis that the partnership stopped trading and started again when you took on new partners. Incoming partners should confirm the partnership's mandate with the bank and should be joined as co-sureties to the bank guarantee. You may also want to extend their liability to cover contracts with the partnership's existing creditors – by replacing the original contracts which include them – and if they should share in existing book debts.

Companies

Company amalgamations are closely regulated under the Companies and Insolvency Acts and arrangements should only be entered into after you have taken proper legal and financial advice.

Share for share and part cash offers

You can make a bid for a company in return for shares which are distributed to the selling company's shareholders in accordance with their rights. You can also make an offer extended generally to all the shareholders with part payment in your shares and the balance in cash. The offer is usually conditional on the acceptance of at least three-quarters of the shareholders, holding not less than 90 per cent of the shares – because you are usually bound to acquire the remaining 10 per cent on the same terms, unless the court orders otherwise on a shareholder's application. Bids can be confined to one class of shares, if your company already holds nine-tenths of that class of shares. If acceptances exceed the offer, you must take shares, *pro rata,* from all accepting shareholders.

The procedure for mergers and reconstructions involving a new issue of shares at a premium are set out on pages 17–18.

You can transfer assets from one company to another on a tax neutral basis. Transfer is on a no gain/no loss basis and can consist of a disposal of the whole or part of a business to another company as part of a scheme of reconstruction or amalgamation, but the assets must remain within the scope of UK taxation.

There is a 0.5 per cent Stamp Duty on sales of shares and other securities, but there are reliefs for certain company reorganisations where there is no significant change of underlying ownership.

Straightforward exchange of shares between buying and selling companies, when you are not seeking further capital, is usually done by issuing your shares to the selling company's shareholders. If a majority of the selling company's shareholders accept, the selling company's shares are cancelled, except for any your company is to hold, and the selling company's shareholders receive your shares in payment for theirs. Payment can be in cash instead of shares if the reserve created by cancellation of the shares is capitalised. This is then applied to pay up further shares in the selling company, which are issued to you in place of the cancelled shares. The result is the same as a share-for-share takeover by compulsory acquisition but the majority necessary to approve the takeover is smaller and the court, creditors and shareholders must approve the arrangement.

Taking over while raising capital

If you are seeking more capital, the selling company must be wound up and its shareholders must make further contributions of capital. A new company is formed and the selling company sells its undertaking through its liquidator in return for shares in the new company. Shareholders receive your shares or they can be given partly paid-up shares in return for the fully paid shares they previously held which means they take on a fresh liability for calls or give up their rights to the new shares.

Varying shareholders' and creditors' rights

Three-quarters of the shareholders or creditors – in number and value – must consent if their rights are to be varied. They can object within 21 days to the court, which can amend, vary, confirm or overrule the scheme. A selling company wanting to persuade its shareholders or creditors to agree to a sale must also apply to the court. The court monitors both these procedures and can order compensation for dissenting shareholders.

Directors' compensation for loss of office

Directors' compensation for loss of office must be approved by the selling company's shareholders or as specified in the Articles, otherwise the directors are liable to prosecution and the compensation belongs to shareholders, even if payment is made within a year before, or two years after, the takeover offer. The first £30,000 is not taxable and a reduced rate of tax applies up to £50,000. Tax is payable at the full rate on the balance. Payments for shares to directors exceeding the price paid to other shareholders are also considered to be compensation, unless the bid is only for de facto control by acquisition of less than a third of voting shares, when the directors are not accountable to shareholders, although they may be liable to the company. They can, however, keep genuine payments for premature determination of service contracts or as a pension for past services.

Statutory references

Companies Act 1985 and 1989
Employment Protection (Consolidation) Act 1978
Income and Corporation Taxes Act 1970 (as amended)
Insolvency Act 1986
Partnership Act 1890
Registration of Business Names Act 1916

Appendix: Useful addresses

British Franchise Association
Thames View
Newton Road
Henley-on-Thames
Oxfordshire RG9 1HG
Tel: 01491 578 050
Web site: www.british-franchise.org.uk

British Insurance Brokers Association
BIBA House
14 Bevis Marks
London EC3A 7NT
Tel: 020 7623 9043
Web site: www.biba.org.uk

Centre for Dispute Resolution
Princes House
95 Gresham Street
London EC2V 7NA
Tel: 020 7600 0500

Companies House Addresses
English/Welsh companies
Companies House
Crown Way
Cardiff CF14 3UZ
Tel: 0870 333 3636/029 2038 0801
Web site: www.companies-house.org.uk

There are also offices in Birmingham, Leeds and Manchester

Scottish companies
Companies House
37 Castle Terrace
Edinburgh EH1 2EB
Tel: 0870 333 3636

Companies House
7 West George Street
Glasgow G2 1BQ
Tel: 0870 333 3636

Data Protection
Registration Office
Wycliffe House
Water Lane
Wilmslow
Cheshire SK9 5AF
Tel: 01625 545745
Web site: www.dataprotection.gov.uk

Department for Education
and Skills
Sanctuary Buildings
Great Smith Street
London SW1P 3BT
Tel: 020 7273 3000
Web site: www.dfes.gov.uk

**Department of Trade
and Industry**
1 Victoria Street
London SW1H 0ET
Tel: 020 7215 5000
Web site: www.dti.gov.uk

**Export Credits
Guarantee Department**
2 Exchange Tower
PO Box 2200
Harbour Exchange Square
London E14 9GS
Tel: 020 7512 7000

**The Health and
Safety Executive**
Rose Court
2 Southwark Bridge
London SE1 9HS
Tel: 0870 154 5500
Web site: www.hse.gov.uk

HPI Ltd
Dolphin House
PO Box 61
New Street
Salisbury
Wiltshire SP1 2TB
Tel: 01722 422422

**Institute of Trade
Mark Agents**
4th floor
Canterbury House
2–6 Sydenham Road
Croydon
Surrey CRO 9XE
Tel: 020 8686 2052

Insurance Ombudsman
South Quay Plaza
183 Marsh Wall
London E14 9SR
Tel: 0845 600 6666

Land Charges Registry
Land Charges Department
DX 8249, Search Section
Burrington Way
Plymouth
PL5 3LP
Tel: 01752 635600
Web site: www.landreg.gov.uk

The Law Society
113 Chancery Lane
London WC2A 1PL
Tel: 020 7242 1222

**Registry of County
Court Judgments**
173–175 Cleveland Street
London W1T 6QR
Tel: 020 7380 0133

Small Business Service
St Mary's House
Moorfoot
Sheffield S1 4PQ
Tel: 0114 259 7788

**Trade Marks, Patents and Design Registry/
The Trade Mark Enquiries Section**
The Patent Office
Concept House
Cardiff Road
Newport NP10 8QQ
Tel: 01663 814000

The Patent Office/The London Filing Facility
Harmonsworth House
13–15 Bovary Street
London EC4Y 8DD
Tel: 08459 500505

Index

Business Enterprise Guides

The Business Enterprise Handbook: A complete guide to achieving profitable growth for all entrepreneurs and SMEs
Colin Barrow, Robert Brown and Liz Clarke

The Business Plan Workbook, Fourth Edition
Colin Barrow, Paul Barrow, Robert Brown

E-Business for the Small Business: Making a profit from the Internet
John G Fisher

Financial Management for the Small Business, Fifth Edition
Colin Barrow

Forming a Limited Company: A practical guide, Seventh Edition (forthcoming)
Patricia Clayton

Running a Home Based Business, Second Edition (forthcoming)
Diane Baker

Starting a Successful Business, Fourth Edition
Michael J Morris

Successful Marketing for the Small Business: A practical guide, Fifth Edition
Dave Patten

The above titles are available from all good bookshops. To obtain further information, please contact the publisher at the address below:

Kogan Page Ltd
120 Pentonville Road
London N1 9JN
Tel: 020 7278 0433
Fax: 020 7837 6348
www.kogan-page.co.uk